Basic Witchery 101

The Moon/Goddess Connection: Because its energy is feminine in quality, the Goddess is often symbolized by the phases of the Moon. Each phase vibrates differently and corresponds to a specific Goddess personality, as well as to a variety of magical purposes.

Waxing Moon/Light Maiden: When the Moon grows from light to full, we use its energies for anything that requires increase, growth, or enhancement. It's a good time to work magic involving inspiration, new love and friendships, financial prosperity, healing, increasing physical stamina, and garden planting.

Full Moon/Mother: The Moon's energy is at its most potent when it reaches this stage. And while we can use it to boost any effort, it's of real benefit to especially complicated workings or difficult situations.

Waning Moon/Dark Maiden: When the Moon shrinks from full to dark, we use its vibration for anything that we want to diminish or eliminate. This energy works well for efforts that involve dieting, breaking bad habits, and eliminating stress or depression.

Dark Moon/Crone: Some practitioners use this phase to rest, regenerate, and regroup. Others use its energies for psychic work, divination, and delving into past life memories.

About the Author

Dorothy Morrison is a Wiccan High Priestess of the Georgian Tradition. She founded the Coven of the Crystal Garden in 1986. An avid practitioner of the Ancient Arts for more than twenty years, she spent many years teaching the Craft to students throughout the United States and Australia and is a member of the Pagan Poet's Society.

An archer and bow hunter, Dorothy regularly competes in outdoor tournaments and holds titles in several states. Her other interests include tarot work, magical herbalism, stonework, and computer networking.

To Write to the Author

If you wish to contact the author or would like more information about this book, please write to the author in care of Llewellyn Worldwide and we will forward your request. Both the author and publisher appreciate hearing from you and learning of your enjoyment of this book and how it has helped you. Llewellyn Worldwide cannot guarantee that every letter written to the author can be answered, but all will be forwarded. Please write to:

Dorothy Morrison
℅ Llewellyn Worldwide
P.O. Box 64383, Dept. 1-56718-446-4
St. Paul, MN 55164-0383, U.S.A.

Please enclose a self-addressed stamped envelope for reply,
or $1.00 to cover costs. If outside U.S.A., enclose
international postal reply coupon.

Many of Llewellyn's authors have websites with additional information and resources. For more information, please visit our website at http://www.llewellyn.com.

INCLUDES RITUALS, SPELLS, AND WICCAN ETHICS

THE CRAFT

A WITCH'S BOOK OF SHADOWS

DOROTHY MORRISON

FOREWORD BY RAYMOND BUCKLAND

2001
Llewellyn Publications
St. Paul, Minnesota 55164-0383, U.S.A.

FIRST EDITION
First Printing, 2001

Cover design by Lisa Novak
Interior illustrations © 2001 by Kate Thomssen

Library of Congress Cataloging-in-Publication Data
Morrison, Dorothy, 1955–
        The craft: a witch's book of shadows / Dorothy Morrison.
            p.   cm.
        Includes bibliographical references.
        ISBN 1-56718-446-4
        1. Witchcraft. I. Title.
        BF1566.M74   2001
299—dc21   2001029063

Llewellyn Worldwide does not participate in, endorse, or have any authority or responsibility concerning private business transactions between our authors and the public.

All mail addressed to the author is forwarded but the publisher cannot, unless specifically instructed by the author, give out an address or phone number.

Any Internet references contained in this work are current at publication time, but the publisher cannot guarantee that a specific location will continue to be maintained. Please refer to the publisher's website for links to authors' websites and other sources.

Portions of this book contain herbal remedies, recipes, and suggestions for magical use. The purpose of this book is to provide educational, cultural, and historical information for the general public concerning herbal remedies that have been used for many centuries. In offering information, the author and publisher assume no responsibility for self-diagnosis based on these studies or traditional uses of herbs in the past. Some herbs and remedies discussed in this book involve toxic or potentially dangerous materials, and the publisher takes no position on the beliefs or effectiveness of methods or treatments discussed in *The Craft*.

A Division of Llewellyn Worldwide, Ltd.
P.O. Box 64383, Dept. 1-56718-446-4
St. Paul, MN 55164-0383, U.S.A.
www.llewellyn.com

Printed on recycled paper in the United States of America

To Nancy Mostad, who spawned this idea, gave it energy, and believed in my ability to write it . . .
and . . .
To my husband, Mark, whose love and gentle support allows me the freedom to be who I am, regardless of whom others think I should be.

In Memory of
My mother, Laura Belle Potter, who charmed all in her path
with the magic of rhyme,
and to her great aunt and first Poet Laureate of Texas,
Mary Hunt Affleck, whose talent ran deep in her veins.

CONTENTS

Acknowledgments   xiii
Foreword   xv
A Note to the Reader   xvii

PART ONE: BASIC WITCHERY
Walking the Path   3
Working with Major Power Sources   13
Boosting the Magic   29

PART TWO: TOOLS OF THE TRADE
Magical Tools   55
The Wand   57
The Cup   69
The Athame   75
The Pentacle   83
Other Tools and Ritual Accoutrements   91
The Ultimate Magical Tool   97

PART THREE: CIRCLE MAGIC
The Circle   109

PART FOUR: WE'RE HAVING A PARTY
The Celebrations   129
The Esbats   131
The Sabbats   153

Afterword   177
Appendix A: Common Dream Symbols   179

Appendix B: The Magical Uses of Herbs,
    Plants, Flowers, and Trees   185
Appendix C: The Magical Uses of Stones   189
Appendix D: Deity Associations   193
Appendix E: The Book of Law   197
Appendix F: Mail Order Supply Stores   205
Suggested Reading List   207
Index   211

ACKNOWLEDGMENTS

MAGIC—OFTEN DEFINED AS the change of any condition by ritual means—is a fascinating process. It takes focus, concentration, and tremendous desire. It involves a ritual of sorts which we gladly perform. Then we wait. Nothing seems to happen. And then when we least expect it—*poof!*—our dreams materialize. We don't always know exactly how it happened. But we can't argue with the fact that it did.

Such was the case with this book. And while I sat at the computer—performing the writer's ritual—other people provided the "how" that made *The Craft* materialize. For this reason, the following folks deserve very special thank-yous.

To Bobbie, Randy, Herb, and Katrina, and all of the other Georgians who went to great pains to teach me that by walking my talk and reaching for my dreams, I could change my own reality—and the world in which I live.

To Cindy Nicola and InaRae Ussack, whose constant support, gleeful attitudes, and incredible knack for making me laugh did more than they'll ever know to get me through this project.

To Trish, Sirona, A. J., Murv, and Karri, who always knew when I needed a break, needed a smile, or just a long-distance hug or two.

To the Acquisitions Dream Team—Nancy Mostad, Ann Kerns, Barbara Wright, and Megan Atwood—whose knack for slaying dragons and waving off problems with the flick of a wand is simply beyond compare.

To Karin Simoneau, Editing Sorceress, whose gentle magic always makes me look good in print, and whose levels of patience and understanding never fail to amaze me.

To the Publicity, Sales, and Marketing departments who carefully sprinkle each book with their own special enchantments.

To Sandra and Carl Weschcke, for believing that knowledge and information—no matter how controversial—is too important to go unshared, and for continually inspiring me to reach for the Moon and grab what it has to offer.

And finally, to every person—young, old, and in-between—who's ever written with a request for spiritual teaching, or asked for a starting point: It's because of you, and your unsinkable search for magical knowledge, that this book even exists.

FOREWORD

IN THE 1930S, IN ENGLAND, the late Dr. Gerald Brousseau Gardner stumbled upon a living coven of Witches and learned the true meaning of Witchcraft. He found that far from being Satanists and devil worshippers, practitioners of black magic and workers of evil, Witches were a benign people closely attuned to nature, whose first and only commandment was to harm none. Gardner confirmed theories put forth by Dr. Margaret Murray, among others, and was the first to stand up for the Witches and speak as one of them, finally presenting their side of the story.

Since that time, others have spoken out in order to dismantle the popular misconceptions about Witchcraft and to show that it is no more than the continuation of an old Pagan religion. In recent years there have been many books expounding on the beliefs and practices of the Witches, or Wicca, revealing that there are many different paths, or traditions, within its structure. Some authors have detailed the rituals while others have concentrated on the magical practices.

Recently there has been a great increase in the popular awareness of the Craft, mainly due to movies and television shows. Most of these, though not totally authentic, are accurate enough to relay the sufficient flavor of Witchcraft, and many people are being drawn to investigate further. But where can people go from there? To books. It is only by the production of such books as *The Craft* that seekers are able to get a true image of what Witchcraft really is, and to correct errors that the media has made.

Witchcraft is not a group of teenagers sitting around trying to cast spells. It is a serious religion for people of all ages, a religion with belief in and worship of deities, a religion closely aligned with Nature. Any magic is secondary to that worship and is only performed when there is a real need for it. When there *is* that need, then the magic must be performed correctly in order to work and to not harm anyone. *The Craft* is a much-needed compendium of Wiccan and magical practices that will help explain and establish the Craft and end much of the bias and misinformation that has gone before.

In *The Craft,* Dorothy continues this enlightenment in an easy-to-read, easy-to-understand format that leads the inquirer through such basics as forming the Circle, celebrating the Sabbats, and making the tools. She emphasizes that the Craft—Witchcraft—is not for everyone, and that it is a serious religion. Without dwelling on the makeup of covens, or the hierarchy, she does stress the *responsibility* of being a Witch. She presents good, basic, down-to-earth advice based on her own experiences. This is a book that is especially useful for the solitary practitioner.

One point that I am delighted to see stressed is the use of rhyme in magic. Rhythm and beat are two main essentials for its success, yet they are frequently glossed over. Here, not only are they brought out, but Dorothy's examples are well defined, with excellent rhyme and flawless meter. She also highlights meditations and gives complete explanations of all that she touches on. To round out the volume, Dorothy includes complete sets of a variety of tables in the appendices, along with sources for materials and a basic reading list. This is one spectacular Witch's "Book of Shadows"—a workbook of Wicca.

RAYMOND BUCKLAND

A NOTE TO THE READER

ALL TEACHING TOOLS INVOLVE a variety of problem-solving exercises. And as much as we don't like thinking about them, they're important. Why? Because without them, there wouldn't be any way to prompt the knowledge we've accumulated. We'd never learn to put our abilities to use or test our strategies in a challenging situation. More important, though, we'd have no way of knowing whether or not we were making any progress. That being the case, it's only fair to warn you that I've included some of those head-scratching exercises in this book, too.

Most of the exercises found here follow the sections on individual magical tools, and mastering them is essential to your practice. It's only through their successful completion that you can come to understand each tool and learn to use it to full magical capacity. For this reason, work with each exercise until it becomes second nature.

To give you a starting point, I've divided the exercises into weeks. This certainly does not mean that you're expected to completely master any exercise listed within a seven-day time frame. (Some exercises are more difficult and take longer than others.) Just work at your own pace and don't get discouraged. Remember that practice makes perfect, and that your magic is only as good as the effort you're willing to put into it.

PART ONE

BASIC WITCHERY

Nails, snails, and dragon's tails:
Are they good for that which ails?
Eye of gnewt and wing of bat:
Will they work for this or that?
All recipes, good Witches know
Are followed to the tip of toe.

A pinch too much? A slip up there?
And Fuzzy Wuzzy has no hair!
Instead of fairies flitting free,
You've conjured up a chimpanzee!
And though he's fun and likes to play—
How do you make him go away?

This is a cookbook for my Craft
Full of giggles, smiles, and laughs!
Concoctions, spells, and recipes
Woven well by Blessed Be's
And designed without one nervous twitch
By one who's proud to be called "Witch!"

Taken from the title page of Dorothy Morrison's personal Book of Shadows

WALKING THE PATH

The Craft is accepting, generous, and loving. It's gentle, unobtrusive, and supportive. It's an ethical way of life that, once embraced, brings immeasurable joy and wonder to everyday living.

Wicca: The Religion

The Craft[1] is not for everyone. It's not for people with chips on their shoulders or beefs against Christianity. It's not for folks who ride high on power trips or step on others to achieve success. It's not for bigots, or braggarts, or those too big for their britches. It simply isn't built that way.

Neither is it a role-playing game. It has nothing to do with canned magic, or flying through the air, or snapping lightning from your fingertips. You won't be able to walk through mirrors without hurting yourself, or make thousands of dollars materialize in the split-second snap of your fingers. And, no matter how hard you try or how practiced you are, it won't give you the power to turn your enemies into frogs so you can set them on the highway. That sort of stuff doesn't happen in real life. It's better left to the movies.

So, if the Craft isn't any of these things, what is it, exactly? The Craft is accepting, generous, and loving. It's gentle, unobtrusive, and supportive. It's an ethical

---

1. The Craft is a commonly used term for Wicca.

way of life that, once embraced, brings immeasurable joy and wonder to everyday living. Simply put, the Craft is a serious religion.

I can almost hear the questions rolling around in your head now. In fact, I'm willing to bet that you're wanting to know about Witches and spells and magic and such. And if I were in your shoes, I would, too.

True enough, practitioners of the Craft often call themselves Witches. That's because the word "witch" stems from the Anglo Saxon word *wicce,* which means "wise one" or "sorceress." "Wicca"—the name of the religion they embrace—is also derived from that word.[2] That being the case, it stands to reason that Wiccans—both male and female—might identify themselves as Witches. It's much the same as followers of Judaism calling themselves Jews, and has nothing to do with pointed hats, missing teeth, or evil spirits.

Magic, on the other hand, is defined as the change of any condition by ritual means. It's nothing more than a simple matter of channeling focused energy toward a specific goal. In fact, Christians do it all the time. They pray for something and they get it. Whether God answers their prayers or not is anybody's guess, but one thing is for sure—a prayer that brings wants and wishes to fruition contains at least four components: intent, focus, concentration, and a hefty dose of strong will. And those are precisely the components necessary for successful results in spellcasting.

Now that we have that out of the way, let's talk a little bit about Wicca, the religion. Although there are some differences, it has a lot in common with Christianity. Like Christianity, for example, Wicca has different religious sectors. We call them traditions, or trads. There are more of these than you can shake a stick at, and new ones crop up every day. Some of the more common trads are Dianic, Gardnerian, Alexandrian, Hereditary, and Family Trad. I belong to the Georgian Trad, a very eclectic group whose teachings are based in Gardnerianism and Alexandrianism with Celtic leanings.

Like Christians, we believe in the Triad of Divinity, but there's a bit of a twist here. Since Wicca is a matriarchal religion, we worship the Triple Goddess; more specifically, the Goddess in Her phases of Maiden, Mother, and Crone. A good many of us also worship Her male counterpart, the Triple God. Because I believe

---

2. This derivation is commonly accepted by most etymologists. Some claim, however, that "Wicca" comes from "wicker," which means "to bend," while others say that it is a new usage of the ancient Norse word "Wicca"—a collective term for the healers of that time period.

in the duality of Godhead (meaning that God is both male and female), I fall into the latter category. My trad extends this belief one step further, though. It teaches that the Goddess rules the seasons of spring and summer, while the God holds dominion over the fall and winter. This not only brings a sort of balance to our Wheel of the Year, but reminds us that as children of the Lord and Lady—the dual Godhead—we are equals, and when it comes right down to it, none of us is more important than the other. We all play major roles in the Universal scheme of things.

Although the movie industry has led many folks to believe otherwise, Wiccans, like Christians, have a code of ethics. Instead of ten commandments to guide us through life, though, we only have one. It is simply this: "And it harm none, do what you will." Adhered to strictly, this rule encompasses everything in the Christian guidelines and more. It keeps us mindful that every action we take—every word we say and every thought we think into fruition—is similar to ripples on a pond, one working its way into the others. Our actions affect the lives of other people; so much so, in fact, that we must take great care not to harm another living soul emotionally, mentally, physically, or on any other level. It's a pretty tall order.

All that having been said, there are also some distinct differences. For one thing, Wicca is an Earth religion, and instead of worshipping within the confines of a church building, we often hold our rituals outdoors. We celebrate the changing of the seasons and the beauty of the Moon, the Stars, and the Sun. We live in harmony with Nature, and believe that all things—even inanimate objects such as stones—have a life and spirit and purpose equal to our own.

We don't believe in the devil, or sin, or hell, or fire and brimstone. It's not that we don't acknowledge the fact that evil exists in the world or that it must be dealt with. We do. It's just that we believe that humankind creates its own evil, and that such horrors are handled through the Laws of Karma and the lessons of reincarnation rather than through exile to a fiery pit. After all, having to repeat our life lessons until we get them right is much more revolting than spending the rest of our lives in a hot place with the possibility of a few blisters!

We believe in the Threefold Law[3] and its justice. This has to do with cause and effect. What this means is that every action taken and every deed performed—whether good or bad—is calculated by karma at triple value, then sent back to us.

---

3. The Threefold Law is also known in many circles as Karmic Law.

5

And though we might be thrilled at the prospect of a threefold return on a good deed, could we stand the amount of aggravation due from poor behavior? Probably not. For that reason, we're really careful about what we do and how we act. It makes us better human beings.

We believe that the world we live in—and the Universe that envelops us—is structured on a system of checks and balances. This means that there must be an equal amount of positive for negative, male for female, joy for sorrow, and so forth—for without checks and balances, our world would become a very unbalanced place. We do not believe, however, that it's Gods' or Goddess' will when something terrible happens or when things don't go according to plan. We just know that it's the Universe's way of putting things right. And though we may not like it, we live with it and go on. No one ever said that life was fair—or that the big picture was always apparent at the onset. We strive to live in perfect love and perfect trust.

We also believe that we are perfectly capable of handling whatever comes our way, and that we have the tools and the power to change our personal realities; that we can be whomever or whatever we want to be and hold any station in life that appeals to us. This means, of course, that we must be totally accountable for ourselves, the goals we reach for, and the paths that we choose to follow. That being the case, though, we have no one to blame but ourselves when things go awry or get out of hand. It's an enormous amount of responsibility.

Wicca isn't nearly as mysterious as most folks think—especially once they realize that the magic involved comprises only the ritualistic part of the big picture. Just like other religions, it involves work, devotion, and application to everyday living, as well as responsible thinking, action, and behavior. What follows in this book is a basic set of instructions, theories, and ideas geared to teach you the Craft and aid you in discovering its many wonders. As you read and learn, just remember that the Craft is not for everyone. If, after thorough exploration, you discover that Wicca is for you, I can promise that you'll never have need to seek an alternative path. Once and for all, you'll be home!

Walking the Path

There are many things involved in walking the path of Wicca effectively. First and foremost, we must remember the things that our parents tried to instill within us.

Things like playing nice, using good judgment, and knowing when to listen rather than speak. But the most important thing is something your parents constantly impressed upon you day in and day out. It, of course, is good manners.

Whether dealing with the deities, members of your Craft family, or just people on the street, these things are important. Sadly enough, though, they seem to be lacking in many of those who live in our world today. For that reason, we live by the tenets listed below. Study them and learn them well. And if a situation arises that isn't covered, just go back to the basics that your parents tried to teach you: If it's not polite, don't do it!

Rede of the Wicca

The Wiccan Rede has been around for a long time. It not only outlines our rules, but gives a brief summary of how we live the magical life. This is important stuff; so important, in fact, that I've always had my students commit it to memory. Memorizing this will serve *you* well, too.

Bide the Wiccan Law you must, in perfect love and perfect trust.

Live and let live; fairly take and fairly give.

Cast the Circle thrice about, to keep all evil spirits out.

To bind the spell every time, let the spell be spake in rhyme.

Soft of eye and light of touch, speak little and listen much.

Deosil go by the waxing Moon, sing and dance the Witches' Rune.

Widdershins go when the Moon doth wane, and werewolf howls by the dread wolfsbane.

When the Lady's Moon is new, kiss thy hand to Her times two.

When the Moon rides at Her peak, then your heart's desire speak.

Heed the Northwind's mighty gale, lock the door and drop the sail.

When the wind comes from the South, love will kiss thee on the mouth.

When the Westwind blows o'er thee, departed spirits restless be.

Nine woods in the cauldron go, burn them fast and burn them slow.

Elder be the Lady's tree—burn it not, or cursed be!

When the Wheel begins a turn, let the Beltane fires burn.

When the Wheel hath turned to Yule, light the log and let Pan rule.

Heed ye flower, bush, and tree, and by the Lady, Blessed Be!

Where the rippling waters flow, cast a stone and truth you'll know.

Whenever ye have a need, harken not to others' greed.

With the fool, no seasons spend, nor be counted as his friend.

Merry Meet and Merry Part, bright the cheeks and warm the heart.

Mind the Threefold Law ye should, three times bad an' three times good.

When misfortune is enow, wear the Blue Star on your brow.

True in love ever be, unless thy love is false to thee.

Eight words the Wiccan Rede fulfill: "An' it harm none, do what ye will!"

The Witches' Creed

"To Know,
to Dare,
to Will,
to keep Silent;
these are the four words of the Magus.
In order to Dare, we must Know
In order to Will, we must Dare.
We must Will to possess empire.
To reign, we must be Silent."

To Know: We must free our minds and clear them of useless clutter, garbage, and worn-out notions. Only then can we open them to accept the gifts of knowledge and truth—the gifts of the Ancients—that await us.

To Dare: We must dare to overcome our own personal ignorance and outdated beliefs. Only then will we gain the personal strength necessary to walk the path of the Craft.

To Will: Without personal will, our magic comes to naught. In order for our efforts to reach success, we must want our goals so badly that we become one with them.

To Keep Silent: This is a twofold matter. First, we must acquire the trait of inner peace and quiet, and cultivate it well within ourselves. Only then can we hear the messages of the Gods, or hear the truth within. The second matter is a mundane one. Unfortunately, bigoted, frightened people still live in our world, and we must understand that those who do not wish to be educated will not be. For that reason, silence is often necessary to protect ourselves and the ways of the Craft.

Thirteen Principles of Wiccan Belief

As simple and unassuming as it is, the Craft is probably more maligned and misunderstood than any other religion on the face of the Earth. And to a large degree, the movie media of years gone by is to blame. They often depicted Witches as mean, hateful, evil people who worshipped the devil, ran amuck, and wreaked untold havoc in the lives of others. Of course, nothing could be further from the truth. Be that as it may, though, a good portion of society not only relished these ideas, but served them up as gospel truth.

In 1974, the Council of American Witches decided to do something about this. They adopted the following principles to define the Craft and help its members live more easily within societal measures. These principles still shape and guide our lives today. (The Thirteen Principles of Wiccan Belief were drafted by Gnosticus, former Chairman of the Council of American Witches. We know this man today as Carl Llewellyn Weschcke, the owner and publisher of Llewellyn Worldwide.)

1. We practice rites to attune ourselves with the natural rhythm of life forces marked by the Phases of the Moon and Seasonal Quarters and Cross-Quarters.

2. We recognize that our intelligence gives us a unique responsibility toward our environment. We seek to live in harmony with Nature, in ecological balance offering fulfillment to life and consciousness within an evolutionary concept.

3. We acknowledge a depth of power far greater than is apparent to the average person. Because it is far greater than ordinary, it is sometimes called "supernatural," but we see it as lying within that which is naturally potential to all.

4. We conceive of the Creative Power in the Universe as manifesting through polarity—as masculine and feminine—and that this Creative Power lives in all people and functions through the interaction of the masculine and feminine. We value neither above the other, knowing each to be supportive of the other. We value sex as pleasure, as the symbol and embodiment of life, and as one of the sources of energies used in magical practice and religious worship.

5. We recognize both outer worlds and inner, or psychological worlds—sometimes known as the Spiritual World, the Collective Unconscious, the Inner Planes, and so on—and we see in the interaction of these two dimensions the basis for paranormal phenomena and magical exercises. We neglect neither dimension for the other, seeing both as necessary for our fulfillment.

6. We do not recognize any authoritarian hierarchy, but do honor those who teach, respect those who share their greater knowledge and wisdom, and acknowledge those who have courageously given of themselves in leadership.

7. We see religion, magic, and wisdom-in-living as being united in the way one views the world and lives within it—a worldview and philosophy-of-life that we identify as Witchcraft, the Wiccan Way.

8. Calling oneself "Witch" does not make a Witch—but neither does heredity itself, or the collecting of titles, degrees, and initiations. Witches seek to control the forces within themselves that make life possible in order to live wisely and well, without harm to others, and in harmony with Nature.

9. We acknowledge that it is the affirmation and fulfillment of life, in a continuation of evolution and development of consciousness, that gives meaning to the Universe we know, and to our personal role within it.

10. Our only animosity toward Christianity, or toward any other religion or philosophy-of-life, is to the extent that its institutions have claimed to be "the only way" and have sought to deny freedom to others and to suppress other ways of religious practice and belief.

11. As American Witches, we are not threatened by debates on the history of the Craft, the origins of various terms, the legitimacy of various aspects of different traditions. We are concerned with our present, and our future.

12. We do not accept the concept of "absolute evil," nor do we worship any entity known as "Satan" or "the devil," as defined by the Christian Tradition. We do not seek power through the suffering of others, nor do we accept the concept that personal benefit can be only derived by denial to another.

13. We acknowledge that we seek within Nature for that which is contributory to our health and well-being.

Unconditional Love Versus Perfect Love, Perfect Trust, and Harm None

Several decades ago, a book-turned-movie really hit its mark with me. The heroine was probably the first Pagan-flavored character ever to receive high acclaim on the silver screen. She delivered a single one-liner about unconditional love that I'll never forget: "Love means never having to say you're sorry."

I pondered that line for weeks. Months. It came back again and again to haunt me. I remember the impression it made on my friends, and how they put its advice into immediate practice. Little by little, their manners slipped. Common courtesy fell by the wayside. Why? Because in their hurry to practice unconditional love, they missed the whole point. Unfortunately, a lot of other people did, too.

Unconditional love is *not* perfect love and has nothing to do with manners or common courtesy. All it means is that you love someone no matter what they do—but it doesn't mean that you like them. It doesn't mean that your feelings haven't been hurt by what they've done or that your life hasn't been impacted adversely by their actions. To love unconditionally doesn't mean that you can continue to be in harmony with someone or that you can ever learn to trust them again. All it means is that you love them in spite of their behavior. And that doesn't breed perfect love and perfect trust. It breeds disharmony, bitterness, and unbridled anger.

For that reason, strive to embrace the three concepts that ground the Wiccan structure:

• Perfect love

• Perfect trust

• Harm none

It's a mighty hefty order. To be able to love perfectly, one must be able to trust and be trusted. In order to trust, one must not harm or be harmed—and that covers a lot of ground.

In short, we must learn to treat others fairly, kindly, and politely. We need to get rid of the "shit happens" attitude and take responsibility for our actions when we screw up. We must learn to say "I was mistaken," "I behaved poorly," and "I'm sorry" with sincerity. We need to exercise a little common courtesy and remember our manners. Yes, we'd risk becoming more refined, more cultured, and perhaps by some definitions, lose some of our freedom. However, we'd also become happier people, feel better about ourselves, and get back into harmony with the rhythms of the Earth. And that's what walking the Wiccan path is truly all about.

WORKING WITH MAJOR POWER SOURCES

Although the deities are always at the center, we also incorporate other factors—the Sun, the Moon, and the Elements—into the pool.

EVERY RELIGIOUS SECTOR IN the world—Christianity, Judaism, or Buddhism, to name a few—is a direct product of its spiritual energy pool. Their members draw from it. Bask in it. They use it to its best advantage. Then they sit back, relax, and reap the benefits it offers. The Craft is no exception.

Just like other religions, we reserve center stage for the deities. We praise Them, honor Them, and ask Them for help once in a while. In return, we expect Them to watch over us and guide us as we go about the business of everyday life. Just as with any other religion, we see the deities as our main power source.

If that's so, then what makes our energy pool any different from anybody else's? The simple fact that ours is multifaceted. Although the deities are always at the center, we also incorporate other factors—the Sun, the Moon, and the Elements— into the pool as well. With the addition of these distinctly individual powers and energies, the pool not only gains strength, but becomes a vast source of power that never runs dry. Used properly, it's a powerful tool that few religions can boast.

This section is designed to teach you how to tap into that energy and use it to your best advantage. Study it at length. Learn it well. And before you know it, that power supply we spoke of will be right at your fingertips. All you'll have to do is reach for it.

The Goddess

While the Goddess is known by many names and has many guises, each falls into one of three categories: Maiden, Mother, or Crone. She is all-powerful, all-knowing, and omnipotent. As the Maiden, She is youthful joy, playfulness, and the innocence of first love. As the Mother, She brings us sensuality and desire, the creative forces of life, and serene nurturement. The Crone—or the Wise One, as some folks call Her—is the embodiment of the other two come full circle. She is the Keeper of Justice, tends the scales of karma, and takes us by the hand when the time comes for us to cross into the next life.

Since all birth and death and rebirth stem from the Goddess, She is often invoked and invited to join us during ritual. At that time, we also take a moment to listen as She speaks to us—Her children—through the priestess. This message is commonly known as the Charge of the Goddess.[1]

Rhyming Charge of the Goddess

I am the harmonious tune of the songbird
And the laughter of a gleeful child.
I am the bubbling sound of the running brook
And the scent of the flowers wild.
I am the floating leaf upon the breeze
And the dancing fire in the forest glade.
I am the sweet smell of rains upon the soil
And the rapture of passion when love is made.
I am the germination of seed in the spring
And the ripening of wheat in the Sun.
I am the peaceful depth of the twilight
That soothes the soul when day is done.
I am found in the twinkling of an aged eye . . .
And found in the birth of a newborn pup . . .
Yes . . . Birth and Growth and Death, am I

---

1. There are many adaptations of the Charge of the Goddess and the Charge of the God. I wrote these in verse for the ease of committing them to memory.

I am the gracious Earth, on whom you sup.
I am your Sister, your Mother, the Wise One.
I wrap you gently in the warmth of my love.
That which you seek you shall find within:
Not without . . . not below . . . not above!
Remember always, my children, be reverent
Be gentle, loving, and kind to each other
And hold sacred the Earth and its creatures
For I am the Lady, Creatrix, and Mother!

The God

As with the Goddess, the God has many names and plays many roles—His main function being that of Her Consort. Nonetheless, He, too, is a Triple Deity and is commonly known as the Young Lord, the Father/Horned One/Greenman, and the Ancient One. All-knowing and omnipotent, He is the catalyst that ignites the Life Force of the Goddess and sets the creation process into motion. As the Young Lord, He is the newborn Sun of winter, the golden joy of childhood, and the masculine flirtations and pleasures of adolescence. As the Father/Horned One/Greenman, He is the virile stag in the woods, the fertile seed that activates the greening of the Earth, and the gentle Father on whom we lean. The Ancient One brings us the voice of reason, the strength of knowing, and the power of experience.

Because He is the Lady's Consort and Love—and because of the many roles he plays in our world and lives—he is often invoked during ritual. At that time, He speaks through the priest. His message to us is known as the Charge of the God.

The Rhyming Charge of the God

I am the echo you hear in the forest, deep
And the warmth of the Sun upon your face
I am the ageless sound of the ocean's roar
And the power that's felt in every wild place
I am the wheat that rustles low on the breezes
And the spark that ignites the hearth fire
I am the passion and power and ecstasy
That is reached at the end of desire

15

I am the squirrel who plays games in the treetops
And the young stag who runs wild and free
I am the clatter of hooves on an old gravel road
And the strength of the ancient oak tree
I am found in the wrinkles of the old crippled man
I am found in the child, young and strong
I am found in the joy of the union of love
In the passionate kiss, slow and long
I am your Lover, your Father, the Ancient One.
Take my hand and I'll teach you the Dance
Of the change of the seasons and the eye of the storm
Of fertility, love, and romance
Remember always, my children, be merry
Hear the lilt of my music, so light
And hold sacred My realm and all it sustains
As you dance to My tune in the night

The Moon/Goddess Connection

Because its energy is feminine in quality, the Goddess is often symbolized by the phases of the Moon. Each phase vibrates differently and corresponds to a specific Goddess personality, as well as to a variety of magical purposes. These are outlined below for your convenience.

Waxing Moon (Light Maiden): When the Moon grows from dark to full, we use its energies for anything that requires increase, growth, or enhancement. It's a good time to work efforts involving fresh starts, inspiration, new love, friendships, business-building, and financial prosperity. It also provides suitable conditions for healing, increasing physical stamina, developing psychism, and garden planting.

Full Moon (Mother): The Moon's energy is at its most potent when it reaches this stage. And while we can use it to boost any effort, it's of real benefit to complicated workings or difficult situations.

Waning Moon (Dark Maiden): When the Moon shrinks from full to dark, we use its vibration for anything that requires shrinkage or elimination. This energy works well for efforts that involve dieting, breaking bad habits, obliterating stress or depression, or the elimination of dysfunctional relationship patterns.

Dark Moon (Crone): Some practitioners use this phase to rest, regenerate, and regroup. Be that as it may, others use its energies for psychic work, divination, and delving into past life memories, as well as matters where getting to the truth of a matter is at issue.

The Sun/God Connection

The Sun's energy is warm and direct, uncomplicated and masculine. Unlike the quarterly motion of the Moon, the Sun changes phases several times each day and gives the practitioner unlimited opportunities for immediate spellwork. Even better, the Sun's wide range of properties can be used to handle almost any magical effort normally aided by the Moon.

Sunrise (Young Lord/Newborn Sun): Sunrise provides a good time for efforts involving beginnings, change, and cleansing. It's also beneficial to work that relates to new employment, love, or direction in life. Matters that involve renewing hope and trust, good health, or even mending a broken heart can also benefit from this energy.

Morning (Young Lord/Adolescent): During the morning hours, the energy of the Sun becomes strong and active, so projects that require building, growth, or expansion benefit during this phase. It also provides the perfect energy for expanding upon the positive aspects in your life, resolving situations where courage is necessary, or adding warmth and harmony to your home and relationships. Use it, too, for financial increase or plant magic.

Noon (Horned One/Greenman): The power of the Sun peaks at high noon. That makes it a good time for work pertaining to mental ability, health, and physical energy. It's also great for charging crystals and stones, or metal ritual tools such as athames, censors, and cauldrons.

Afternoon (Father): As the Sun descends, its energy becomes more receptive in nature. For this reason, use it for efforts involving professionalism, business matters, communications, and clarity. It's also beneficial to matters of discovery, exploration, or travel.

Sunset (Ancient One): This is the time to work on anything that requires reduction or alleviation. Try it for removing stress, anxiety, confusion, hardship and depression, the disclosure of deception, and dieting.

Dealing With the Deities

Because we are a reflection of the Gods and They are a reflection of us, it stands to reason that They might have a few weaknesses. These are not the types of weaknesses you might think, though. The simple truth is that They like to be praised. They love to be entertained. They like a formal invitation to ritual, and They simply adore a good dose of flattery. That's not so bad. We enjoy all those things, too.

So it stands to reason that when dealing with the Gods, it pays to give Them what They like. After all, how willing would you be to help someone who wasn't appreciative enough to tell you how wonderful you were once in a while? Truth be told, you'd probably think twice about it. And that's exactly what you want to prevent.

Here's the deal: You not only want the Gods to be glad to hear from you, you want Them to simply jump at the chance to help you. This means that some form of enticement is in order. You need something to bait Them, lure Them, and tempt Them a little. And the best temptation I know is an appropriate invocation or chant written in couplets.

Couplets—a form of poetry in which the last two words in each pair of lines rhyme—are easy to write. You don't have to be a poet. You don't even need any writing talent. All that's necessary is some paper, something to write with, and a little thought and effort. (A rhyming dictionary comes in handy, too.) When working with protection efforts, for example, you might normally say something like:

Gracious Goddess, protect me from all harm seen and unseen.

When reworked into couplet form, however, the request would read something like:

> *O Gracious Goddess, hear my plea*
> *Protect me from harm I can and can't see*

That was simple enough. And "simple" is the key to writing couplets effectively. They don't have to be fancy; even a little ditty will do. Just remember not to let the words or ideas overwhelm you. The point, after all, is to entice and entertain. And nothing is more entertaining than a jingle or two!

While couplets definitely provide a terrific device for engaging the deities, their power doesn't stop there. In fact, I've discovered that they work wonders in all areas of magic. Here's why:

1. Couplets set the mood. Because they sound magical, they create the proper atmosphere and strengthen goal focus.

2. Couplets flow. Because they roll off the tongue with ease, they provide smooth flight for magical efforts.

3. Couplets have rhythm. Since rhythm transports us into other dimensions, they provide the trancelike state necessary for magical success.

4. Couplets form a spiritual adhesive. They glue the spell together so all components reach their destination intact and at the same time. And that's important for good results.

For these reasons, make an effort to incorporate couplets into all your magical efforts. It's the best way I know to jumpstart your work and gain an edge toward magical success.

One last thing about dealing with the Gods. Unlike some deities worshipped by other religious groups, ours have a great sense of humor. They like to laugh and frolic and have a good time. They also enjoy a good joke now and then, especially when it's at someone else's expense. For that reason, don't get flustered or upset if you accidentally get tongue-tied and flub that glorious invocation you rehearsed so perfectly. Just laugh at yourself and go on. It won't impede your magic, and the Gods will love you just as much as They always did. Maybe even a little bit more.

The Elements[2]

Yellow is the color of Air:
Of winds blown strong and winds blown fair.
Red belongs to flames and Fire,
Burning brightly on the pyre.
If Water is your quest, use blue
Tides rise and fall in azure hue.
The tint of Mother Earth is green . . .
Calm and peaceful and serene.
In your mind, these colors gel:
And they will serve you very well!

The Elements—Air, Fire, Water, and Earth—play a major role in our day-to-day existence. That's because everything on our planet is either comprised of them singularly, or in one combination or another. And because it's an Earth-based religion, the Elements also play an integral part in the rituals, magic, and celebratory processes of Wicca.

Here's how it works. Each Element has two poles or forces: one *active* and the other *passive*. When the Element is in active mode, it works in a positive manner and its energy takes shape in very creative and constructive ways. When the Element is in passive mode, however, its force becomes destructive. This results in negative energy, which, of course, is something we can all do without.

Each Element also has specific scientific qualities or principles. These are important because they make the Elements pull together as a team. In fact, when all the Elements are used in equal combination, they form static electricity. It's something that we not only use daily in technology, but the exact substance we create when we cast a ritual Circle.

There's more. Because we live on the Earth, our bodies are also comprised of a combination of the Elements. This means that each Element rules particular body regions, vital organs, and human functions. When we feel out of sorts or get sick, it's because our *chi* (life force) isn't flowing properly—and this is a direct result of personal Element imbalance.

---

2. My tradition subscribes to the Element colors listed here. Other traditions may use an entirely different set of color correspondences.

Because every Element is different in quality, substance, and principle, I've outlined them separately for your convenience. Study these at length, learn them well, and before long, using the Elements to your best benefit will become second nature. The payoff is well worth the effort.

Fire

Color: Red

Direction: South

Body Rulership: Head, neck, shoulders, and arms

A magical force that we can see and hear flows through the matrix of the Fire Element and brings it to life. We see it in the spark and dance of the flame, and hear it pop and crackle on the hearth fire. Because it reacts similarly to electricity and holds a positive charge, we call this force *electrical fluid*. It relates directly to the expansion qualities of Fire, is red in color, and controls the head, neck, and shoulders.

Fire Polarity Chart

Active		Passive	
Action	Interest	Destruction	Intolerance
Courage	Movement	Devastation	Irritability
Eagerness	Productivity	Gluttony	Jealousy
Enthusiasm	Resolution	Hatred	Overindulgence

Water

Color: Blue

Direction: West

Body Rulership: Abdomen and human emotion

Unlike Fire, magnetic qualities flow through the core of the Water Element. We feel its pull in the current of the river and see it when the tides roll in at the rise of the Moon. This force is called *magnetic fluid*. It holds a negative charge and is directly linked to the cool, shrinking, contracting characteristics of Water.

Water Polarity Chart

Active		Passive	
Compassion	Modesty	Anger	Indifference
Devotion	Nurturement	Bitterness	Selfishness
Forgiveness	Serenity	Depression	Stagnation
Love	Tenderness	Guilt	Timidity

Air

Color: Yellow

Direction: East

Body Rulership: Chest and lungs

Carrying the qualities of both humidity and dryness, the Air Element has a special relationship with the Elements of Fire and Water. It feeds Fire and gives it power. It changes the structural density of Water and turns it into fog, rain, sleet, and snow. But best of all, Air forms a mediatorial bridge, or *electrical ground,* between Fire and Water. This is important because Fire and Water operate independently on opposite poles. The bridge formed by Air, though, gives them an opportunity to mix and mingle, and take shape as steam, smoke, and lightning.

Air Polarity Chart

Active		Passive	
Cheerfulness	Inspiration	Contempt	Indecisiveness
Dexterity	Joy	Fickleness	Ruthlessness
Diligence	Optimism	Gossiping	Sneakiness
Gentleness	Playfulness	Incapacitation	Weakness

Earth

Color: Green

Direction: North

Body Rulership: Feet, legs, and bowels

The Earth Element works independently of Fire, Water, and Air; it contains all of these Elements in their most solid forms. Together they form rock, lava, glaciers, and provide a firm surface for our planet. In various combinations, they also determine the consistency of the soil, making it rich, moist, warm, and dusty. Because Earth actively involves the other three Elements and takes its life source from their combination, we call its force *electromagnetic fluid*.

Earth Polarity Chart

Active		Passive	
Confidence	Respect	Apathy	Inertia
Endurance	Responsibility	Boredom	Pessimism
Patience	Sincerity	Deceit	Tardiness
Punctuality	Tenacity	Distrust	Unreliability

Balancing the Elements Within You

Now that the charts and explanations are out of the way, let's talk a little bit about how the Elements affect us personally. Each human being is, in effect, the Cosmos in miniature. And even though its workings influence us greatly, we, as magical practitioners, also have the ability to influence the Universe. In fact, we are perfectly capable of bending and shaping it any way we like. Before we can do this, though, we have to be absolutely sure that we are in perfect balance. Otherwise, the end result might be anything other than what we expect, and we could wind up really sick.

What does personal Element imbalance have to do with magical work? For one thing, the body has its own set of active and passive poles. In right-handed folks, for example, the right side is electric and active, and the left side is magnetic and passive. (Just the opposite is true of lefties.) The fluids we spoke of earlier travel the channels between these poles and use them to direct energy toward our magical efforts. Because of this, the body is the most important magical tool we possess.

Just as we wouldn't go into battle with a defective weapon, we can't expect to be magically effective unless all of our tools are operating at full tilt boogie. That having been said, let's get started on putting ourselves back in balance.

Knowing Yourself

In order to master the Craft and put things back in balance, we must know ourselves very well. We must be willing to take a good hard look at what makes us who we are. This isn't always pleasant because it's not only a matter of looking at our good qualities; it also means delving into personal characteristics that we're not very proud of. Be that as it may, it's vital to our roles in the Craft to look at the whole picture and set things right within ourselves.

The best way to do this is to make a list of all of your positive and negative qualities. This is not the time to delude yourself. Unless you're totally honest, this exercise will be a complete waste of time! Once you've made the list, write the corresponding Element beside each item. In this way, you'll be able to see where your Elements are unbalanced and take steps to correct it.

Your list should look something like this:

Positive	Negative
Loving: Water	Stubborn: Earth
Compassionate: Water	Lazy: Earth
Generous: Earth	Arrogant: Fire
Enthusiastic: Fire	Vindictive: Fire
Productive: Fire	Irritable: Fire
Patient: Earth	Jealous: Fire

A quick study of the chart above shows an overabundance of Fire and Earth, a lack of Water, and no Air whatsoever. But how do you bring them back into balance? It's not as hard as you might think. All you have to do is try some of the Element strengthening exercises that follow. Only concentrate on the lacking Elements, though. It will help them overpower those in abundance and bring personal balance, in short order.

Air: This Element corresponds to ideas, inspiration, the thought process, and communication. To rectify a lack of this Element, burn some incense, scent your home, your clothes, or your body, write letters or stories, or meditate. You might also try a visit to an art gallery or museum, a friendly game of cards, or dancing to your favorite music. Do something just for fun.

Fire: Fire is a productive, active, enthusiastic Element. To correct a weakness in this area, bake something, sit by the fire, take a walk, or bask in the sunshine. Take some initiative. Tie up loose ends, finish a project you started long ago, or begin a new project that you've never gotten around to.

Water: Since the Water Element corresponds to the emotional realm, it's important to choose activities that you really enjoy. These might include swimming, taking a bubblebath, playing with water guns, walking the shoreline, or wading through a creek. Hug someone you love, have a good, long cry, or toast the Full Moon with a glass of water, then drink it for empowerment.

Earth: To remedy a problem in this area, work outside in the yard, rake leaves, plant flowers, or repot your houseplants. Exercise, play with animals, walk barefoot, or sit under a tree. You'll be grounded before you know it.

Perform the exercises for a month, then make a new list of personal characteristics without looking at the first one. Compare the two when you are finished. Qualities that didn't appear on the first list will be apparent on the new one. You'll also discover that you feel differently about life, situations that arise, and may even be compelled to make some changes in your lifestyle. Don't be alarmed. It just means that you're back in Elemental sync, and are finally seeing your personal world as it really is.

Magical Theory: The Elements

The ability to control and direct the Elements at will is imperative to successful magic, and the exercises that follow are designed to help you do just that. Work each of them with great care, and record your progress daily.

Air Exercise

Using your imagination, put a thought into the air and, as you inhale, absorb the thought into your body. The thought can be anything at all. You may, for example, wish to break a bad habit, study more effectively, or put yourself in a better mood. Begin with seven breaths on the first day, and add one breath each day thereafter. With ten minutes of diligent practice every day, results should be apparent in a week to ten days.

Fire Exercise

Using your imagination, imbue a candle with the same thought used in the exercise above. Light the candle in a dark room, then watch the flame as it fills the area with the light of the thought. Let the candle burn for ten minutes each day, working the exercise for seven to ten days.

Water Exercise

Using your imagination, infuse a bowl of ice water with the same idea used in the exercises above. Wash your hands and face to absorb the thought. Work this exercise for seven to ten days.

Earth Exercise

Using your imagination, impress the same thought you used in the Air exercise upon your daily meals. Holding your hands over the plate, see the thought working its way into your food and saturating every morsel. Concentrating as you eat, consume every bite. Work this exercise for seven to ten days.

Akasha: The First Element

Color: White or Purple

Direction: All and none; the center of the Universe

Body Rulership: The human aura and the brain

Much has been written about Air, Fire, Water, and Earth. Akasha, on the other hand, is an entirely different story. Maybe that's why we often forget about its existence, its function, and the power that it holds for us. And to a Witch, that can spell absolute travesty.

So, what is it, exactly?

Akasha is the first Element. It's the matrix from which all other Elements are born, the core from which they take their power, and the reason for their function in our world. Commonly known as "ether," it forms the basic substance of the Universe at large. Without it, both the spiritual and mundane planes would surely cease to exist as we know them, and magic would just be a passing fancy in the business of day-to-day living. For these reasons, Akasha plays a very important role in the Craft.

Granted, working with an Element that we can't see, feel, smell, or touch might seem like an effort in futility. With a little practice, though, you'll be using it to your best advantage in no time flat! Just work with the following exercises, and record your progress.

Akasha Exercise One

For the next five minutes, let your mind drift while paying close attention to your thought patterns. Try to retain your exact thoughts in their exact order as they traveled through your head. Repeat this exercise daily for at least two weeks.

Akasha Exercise Two

For the next three minutes, concentrate on holding only one thought. Repeat this exercise daily, increasing the time until you can hold one thought for ten minutes.

Akasha Exercise Three

Clear your head, then keep your mind completely blank for the next three minutes. Repeat this exercise daily, increasing the time until you can keep your mind blank for ten minutes.

Prayer to the Elements

This prayer to the Elements works wonders. Said on a daily basis, it not only prevents recurring Element imbalance, but will keep you mindful of the important roles that each individual Element plays in your life.

Come to me Air, so fresh and so clean!
Grant mental power—keep my thoughts sharp and keen!
Bring creativity—bring clarity, too!
Lend your positive aspects to all that I do!
Come to me Water, so flowing and free!
Lend compassion and love and gentility!
Grant understanding—and tempers, please soothe—
And life's little problems, please help me to smooth!
Come to me Fire—so warm and so bright!
As I walk through this life, my pathway, please light!
Please help me to live and to love with pure zest—

Standing up for the Truth, when I'm put to the test!
Come to me Earth, so rich and so moist!
Bestow, please, Your gifts of serene peace and joy!
Grant Your stability and ethical ways,
So I may help others, the rest of my days!
Akasha, please come, and work with these four—
And balance Their aspects within me once more!
Transform my life, for You hold the key
To changing me into that which I should be!
Elements of all that live and shall be,
Please spin your spell in pure harmony—
Weaving the threads of my life with ease,
And stitching its fabric with Blessed Be's!

BOOSTING THE MAGIC

*Boosters even the odds and give our magic that
little something extra to help it along its way.*

THERE'S NO SUCH THING as having too much help. In fact, most of the time we just
don't get enough. Take that dream job, for example. You're definitely qualified,
but no matter what you do, you just can't get an interview. What if someone
opened the door for you? Or maybe just mentioned your name to the right person? You'd probably have that job in a minute. Sometimes, that's all we need. Just
the tiniest bit of help to jumpstart things and set them in motion.

The same is true of magic. At the onset of magical workings, though, we are
usually at more of a disadvantage. This is because we're working with little or
nothing and trying to create something, and bring it to fruition. Sometimes it
works. Sometimes it doesn't.[1] And sometimes, it just fizzles out before it ever
leaves the altar. That's where magical boosters come in. They even the odds and
give our magic that little something extra to help it along its way.

---

1. Magic usually works in twenty-one days, or not at all.

To that end, all the boosters you'll ever need are outlined in this section. Use them individually and try them in combination. See what works for you and what doesn't. And while you're in creation mode, remember to relax and have fun. After all, a stressed Witch is anything but powerful!

Working With the Days of the Week

Let Sunday's sunshine smile on you
And gain success in all you do
On Monday, work on hearth and home
And garden plants that tend to roam
Tuesday is a day of war
Compete today and you'll go far
If inspiration's what you need
Have Mercury's Wednesday plant the seed
For money, luck, and business deals
Let Thursday's planet grease the wheels
For Venusian blessings from above
Use Friday's grace for spells of love
Count lessons learned on Saturday
And karma won't come home to stay
Always work in harmony
(Remember, too, the Law of Three)
Set magic free and let it flow
And watch success rates flex and grow

Since each day of the week is ruled by a different planet—and every planet exudes its own individual energy—most practitioners choose to perform spells on a day that's in sync with their magical intent. While this could postpone the work for a few days, the delay is always well worth the wait. Why? Because matching the intent to the proper planetary influences not only empowers the magic at hand, but to a large degree, eliminates the possibility of Cosmic error.

While that's certainly reason enough to cross-match intent with an appropriate day of the week, my thinking goes one step further. Because performing successful magic is a time-consuming, energy-draining process, it only makes sense to get it right the first time. And there's just no point in wasting precious time and energy if you're working against stacked odds.

A love spell, for example, has little or no chance for success if performed on Tuesday. That's because Tuesday is ruled by Mars, the planet of war. But if you performed it on Friday, its chances would be much better. Why? Because Friday is ruled by Venus, the planet of love. You get the idea.

For this reason, always check the Influences Chart that follows when preparing for magic. Not only will it clear the path for success, but will save you tons of time and energy in the long run. To work in any other way is just like pounding your head against a brick wall!

Influences Chart

Sunday: This day is ruled by the Sun. It provides an excellent energy for efforts involving general success, business partnerships, job promotions, business ventures, and professional success. Magical work involving friendships, joy, and mental or physical health also benefit from this influence.

Monday: Monday belongs to the Moon. Its energy benefits efforts that deal with women, the family, home and hearth, the garden, and medicine. It also boosts rituals involving psychic development and prophetic dreaming.

Tuesday: Mars rules Tuesday. Try it for work involving men, conflict, physical endurance and strength, lust, hunting, sports, and all types of competition. It's also a great tool for rituals that deal with surgical procedures or political ventures.

Wednesday: Wednesday is ruled by Mercury. Its energy is most beneficial to efforts involving writers, poets, actors, teachers, and students. That's because its influences vibrate toward inspiration, communications, the written and spoken word, and all forms of study, learning, and teaching. It also provides a good time to begin efforts that deal with self-improvement or understanding.

Thursday: Jupiter governs Thursday, and influences work that involves material gain, general success, accomplishments, honors and awards, or legal issues. Its energies also benefit matters of luck, gambling, and prosperity.

Friday: Friday belongs to Venus, the planet of love. Since its energies are warm, sensuous, and fulfilling, it's of great benefit to efforts involving matters of the heart, pleasure, comfort, and luxury. Use it, too, for any magical work that deals with music, the arts, or aromatherapy.

Saturday: Saturn, the planet of karma, presides over this day. It provides excellent conditions for efforts that involve reincarnation, karmic lessons, the mysteries, and wisdom. Its energies also benefit any work that deals with the elderly, death, or the eradication of pests and disease.

Candle Colors

Proper colors for a spell
Make them work extremely well.
This list will make your magic strong
So study carefully and long
The candle colors listed here—
And all your spells will bring you cheer!
For lustful love and hot desire,
Use a candle red as fire.
If tranquil peace you now pursue,
Burn a bit of palest blue.
For protection, you may use the same;
Likewise, if your health is lame.
Pink for harmony and love
And perfect union from above.
If to attract is your intent,
Orange is what the heavens sent!
If your hold on things, in time, goes sour—
Use purple to regain your power
To increase your bank account,
Light green candles 'round about.
To ground yourself and make it stick,
Brown candles always do the trick!
To organize, use deepest blue,
For stress relief, a lavender hue.
Use teal for balance, peach for friends
Black puts bad habits at an end.
Use white if you must substitute:
It contains all hues of color suit.

If you burn white instead, it's true,
You must concentrate on proper hue.
Use these wisely. Learn them well
For each and every time you spell,
You weave a dream that you create
Into a realistic state.
The Universe will not say, "No!"
But confusing it may cause you woe!

Color and Its Purpose

Color plays a large part in our world; in fact, nothing else we come into daily contact with impacts us quite as much. It affects the way we feel and act. It affects both our physical and mental energy levels. It even tends to flavor the decisions we make on a day-to-day basis. Marketing firms, for example, use a lot of red and yellow in their advertisements. They know that these colors not only catch the eye, but tend to bring out the buying urge in everyone. Purple makes us think of royalty, while black brings the clergy to mind. And what about people who dress in muted shades? We usually think of them as being more conservative than folks who wear flashy tropical prints.

There's simply no logical basis for the way colors make us feel. They can even cause personal reactions that we don't understand. That's because color tugs at our emotions rather than our sense of reason, and stirs up feelings deep inside. Since it is directly linked to the emotional pool—and successful magic relies heavily upon emotion rather than logic—it's not surprising that it has an intense effect on every magical effort we perform.

The information that follows provides a starting point for using color in magical work. Since everyone is different, though, work with colors on a regular basis and see how they affect you personally. You may even discover that a shade that turns most folks off really trips your trigger—and if that's the case, the discovery could go a long way toward bringing the results you desire.

When working with color, please don't draw the magical line at candle usage. Work with the color of clothing, art objects, and even the sheets you sleep under. Sometimes the most powerful magic of all is right at our fingertips, and we just forget to use it.

Basic Color Chart

Black: Usually associated with the clergy and ministerial figures, black stops gossiping, meddling people right in their tracks. It's also great for breaking bad habits, or for any work that involves separation, wisdom, secrets, or invoking the Crone aspect of the Triple Goddess.

Pale Blue: This shade goes a long way in relieving confusion, anxiety, and loss of control. Try it for efforts that involve calmness, peace, tranquility, healing, and pleasant dreams.

Dark Blue: If you need to get organized and add some structure to your life, this is the color for you. It's also a wonderful hue for invoking the Water Element, or calling upon feminine deities.

Brown: If you tend to bounce off the wall with excess energy, try brown. It works wonders when it comes to grounding and centering, as well as for magical work involving stability and common sense. Try it, too, for diffusing potentially harmful situations.

Gold: Generally used in altar candles to represent the God, gold tends to make us feel financially prosperous and personally secure. I've also found that it's a great perk to efforts involving financial increase and general success.

Green: If you lack ambition, hate challenges, and always feel that you're dependent on someone else, this color can help. Use it, too, for invoking fertility, prosperity, growth, general independence, and the Earth Element.

Lavender: This color is a fabulous tension-reliever, even in the most stressful situations. It's also great for workings that involve the intellect and knowledge retention, controlling erratic energy, and for making inner beauty come to the surface.

Mauve: This color tends to bring cooperation from even the most stubborn of people. It works well in efforts that deal with the increase of intuitive and psychic powers, self-trust, and self-confidence.

Orange: If personal motivation is a problem, try orange. There's nothing quite like it to make you want to get off your duff and take action. It's also great for attraction rituals, gaining positive test scores, and business projects and proposals.

Peach: Because peach is a safe, reassuring color, it works wonders during those times when a gentle, nurturing, and nonthreatening appearance is necessary. It's also a great asset to efforts involving friends, kindness, sympathy, empathy, and well-wishing.

Pink: Because it stimulates self-love, this color can help you to become your own best friend. It also works well in efforts that involve romance, love, friendship, and harmony.

Purple: A terrific color to wear on job interviews, purple helps you gain respect. Try it, too, for work that deals with spirituality, mental and psychic power, and for invoking the Akasha Element.

Red: Especially helpful to shy folks who hold positions of authority, this color really shines when it comes to taking charge of difficult situations. It also works well in efforts that involve passion, sexual desire, vitality, and physical strength, energy, and activity. Use it, too, when invoking the Fire Element or the Mother aspect of the Triple Goddess.

Silver: Commonly used in altar candles to represent the Goddess, this color also works well in rituals to relieve inner turmoil and gain a personal sense of peace and serenity.

Teal: Teal not only brings equal footing to practicality and spirituality, but makes you feel like you can handle even the most insurmountable of problems. Use it in work that deals with getting a handle on practical matters, decision-making, balance, and matters that involve gaining trust.

Turquoise: A must for workaholics, this color forces you to take a step back and look at your workload through new eyes. It works well in rituals that involve stress relief, study, and knowledge retention, and finding logic in situations where none seems to exist.

White: To relieve tension and bring focus to life goals, try white. It's also great for efforts that require clarity or spiritual guidance, and for invoking the Maiden aspect of the Triple Goddess. (*Note:* Since white is a culmination of all colors, it may be substituted for any color during magical work.)

Yellow: Ever feel that no matter how loud you talk, no one hears what you say? If so, then this is the color for you. It works best in efforts dealing with communication, creative endeavors, success, and joy. Use it, too, for invoking the Air Element and the God.

Anointing Candles

It's always a good idea to anoint candles before using them in magic. The reason for this is that it leaves less room for Cosmic error. For one thing, it reminds the candle that it's a magical tool. For another, it gives the candles a specific property. But most important, it puts the candle on notice that once it's burning, it must send your message to the Universe posthaste. And that clears the path to get magic off the ground.

Anointing candles is easy. All you need is an oil appropriate to your intent, or some vegetable oil and a purpose-appropriate herb. (For herb purpose information, see appendix B in the back of this book.) Then follow the instructions below. Your magic will soon be soaring high.

1. Rub a few drops of oil between your palms, then grasp the center of the candle with both hands.

2. Close your eyes and concentrate on magical intent. See the results you desire manifesting in reality.

3. Move your hands slowly toward the ends of the candle while chanting something appropriate to your magical purpose. (Some folks like to use a twisting motion to coat the candle thoroughly.)

4. If you opted for the vegetable oil and herb method, roll the candle in the plant material.

That's all there is to it. The candle is now ready for magical use.

Incorporating Symbols

No matter who we are or where we live, we all understand certain images. Take the heart, for example, the smiley face, or even the handshake. We all know what they mean. That being the case, symbols not only cross cultural boundaries, but comprise the most perfect language in the world.

One of the reasons that symbols impact us so strongly is that they are capable of doing something that most other mediums cannot: They can speak to the subconscious and unconscious minds at the same time, and carry on both conversations successfully. The conscious mind can't help but eavesdrop, and it gets the messages, too. What it hears changes the way it views the world. Before long, we find ourselves looking at things differently, as well.

Take the word "son," for example. The mind immediately conjures up images of a male child. But if we change the word to "Sun," the image changes, also. That's how symbols work. There's no conscious thought or will involved. It's an independent, instantaneous process fueled by multilevel communication. As such, there is nothing that symbols can't do.

That's all well and fine. But what about magic? How do they help us there? When we focus on symbols, the unconscious and subconscious minds take that energy and turn it into a complete list of magical possibilities to forward to the Higher Self. The Higher Self takes a look and decides what we need to reach the desired goal. It then chooses the best course of action and sets the spell in motion. Finally, it simplifies that information and sends it to the conscious mind. And when that happens, we begin to do on a mundane level whatever it takes to bring magical success. The magic takes flight. It gains momentum. Before we know it, the desired result is more than just achievable—it is reality.

Because symbols speak quickly and universally, they not only boost magical work but nearly always bring immediate results. Give them a shot and you'll discover what I did. There's nothing quite like them when it comes to transforming your life into the one you always wanted to live.

The Winds

Winds blown cold and winds blown warm
Gentle breezes with their charm
Stormy gales and hot winds, too
Work their magic just for you
For new beginnings, try the East
Write rituals until it's ceased
The South, it's true, can bring romance
So cast off fears and take a chance

The cleansing West wind soothes and heals
It ties loose ends and clenches deals
Use the North to clear the head
To pad pockets and control the 'stead
Watch the wind and how it blows
Use its power as it flows
To send your magic on the way
In its breezy, dancing play

The winds are part of our everyday life. They cool us, warm us, sometimes even lift our spirits and quicken our steps. And though we seldom give them much thought, winds can do much to increase magical success.

The energy of each wind is unique, and differs according to the direction from which it blows. And since wind gains its magical power from direction rather than force, playful breezes are just as potent as their blustery kin. This is a great perk for practitioners because they don't have to wait for a storm before incorporating them in magic. There's nearly always a wind of some type just waiting to be included.

What if you can't tell which way the wind is blowing? Or what if it's too nasty to go outside and check? Just hang a windsock outside your window. It eliminates guesswork and solves the problem completely.

East Wind: Try this wind when you have a need for change, transformation, new beginnings, and fresh perspective. Since it also provides the perfect environment for inspirational, communicative, and creative ventures, it comes in handy for writing spells and rituals, and talking things over with your Spirit Guide as well.

South Wind: Although this wind is commonly used for magical efforts that deal with love, lust, and passion, its powers don't stop there. It also provides excellent conditions for work involving physical energy, initiative, courage of conviction, and determination, as well as those where resolving anger, jealousy, and selfishness are an issue.

West Wind: This wind has a soothing, healing, cleansing quality, which makes it conducive to issues that involve physical and mental fertility, strengthening the intuition, and the multilevel productivity necessary to tie up loose ends.

North Wind: The cold strength of this wind is hard, fast, and practical. For that reason, it provides the proper atmosphere for efforts that involve finances, business or home management, and clarity of mind. It also makes a good planning period for magical efforts you want to tackle once the wind changes.

Herbs

When it comes to magical work, herbs are more commonly used than any other resident in the plant world. Why? Because they are so strong, so tenacious, and so resilient that no other group of plants even comes close. This inordinate power stems from the fact that herbs are little more than common weeds. And if you've ever tried to keep an army of weeds from infiltrating your precious flower garden, you know exactly what I'm talking about. You can chop them, hoe them, pull them out by the roots, but no matter what you do, they just keep coming back and running amuck until you're at wit's end. Fortunately for the Witch, though, this sort of raw, independent energy can go a long way when harnessed and applied to magical work.

When using herbs in magic, it really doesn't matter whether they're fresh or dried. But it's always a good idea to charge them first. There's good reason for this: It infuses them with the properties you desire, bends them to your will, and causes even the most unruly of the bunch to work in harmony with the effort at hand. Besides, charging herbs is easy and it doesn't take much time. Just follow the directions below. The results will astound you.

Charging Herbs

1. Gather the amount of herb necessary for the current effort and place it in a dish. Hold your hands over the herb until you can feel its energy rise. (You may feel a bit of warmth or even a slight tingle.) Then close your eyes, touch the herb with your dominant hand, and concentrate on your magical intent.

2. Still concentrating on magical intent, scoop up some of the herb and rub it between your hands. This allows your energy to mix with the plant energy. Within a few moments, you'll feel the energies mix and mingle and flow between your hands.

3. Continue to rub the herb between your hands and chant something appropriate to your magical intent. If, for example, you were charging chamomile for a stress-relief ritual, you might say something like:

Herb of pure serenity
Bring your peace and calm to me

Keep chanting until the herb begins to tingle between your palms.

4. Repeat the process with any other herbs you intend to use in that effort.

Using Herbs in Magic

There are more ways to use herbs in magic than you can shake a stick at. For your convenience, I've listed a few of the most popular methods. But don't stop there. Use your imagination and create your own techniques. You may even come up with a trick or two that no one else has thought of!

Burning: To infuse the air with magical intent, toss a bit of dried herb on hot charcoal. Other burning methods include adding herbs to incense or using them to coat anointed candles.

Carrying: Herbs make wonderful charms when carried on you or in your purse. You can even wear them in your hair or lapel if you like. Just a sprig or two appropriate to your purpose will do the trick.

Growing: There's nothing quite like living, growing herbs when it comes to magical work. They provide a constant reminder to the Universe that your magical intent is an ongoing process.

Infusion: This is, perhaps, the most versatile way to use herbs. In fact, the infusion process[2] has a magic all its own since it literally changes dry plant material into liquid form. This opens many windows of opportunity. You can use them as washes to clean the house, rinse your hair with them, add some to the rinse cycle of your laundry, and even drink some of them as tea.[3] Used in oil form, we use infusions to anoint candles, ritual tools, and the most important magical instrument of all: ourselves.

Powdering: For ongoing magic, try powdered herbs in potpourris and sachets. Sprinkle them on carpets, under rugs, and on closet shelves. To make a great body powder, mix them with cornstarch or unscented talcum powder.[4]

Seeding: When change is necessary, toss a few herb seeds on the winds while concentrating on the desired results. Transformation will come as the seeds begin to sprout.

Basic Herb List

While having a large assortment of herbs is handy when it comes to magical use, it just isn't necessary. In fact, you'll probably find most of what you really need already in the kitchen cabinet. If not, though, don't despair. Check appendix B in the back of this book. Part of basic witchery is learning to work with what you have and substitute if need be. A basic herb list follows.

Bay leaf: This is a terrific herb for magical efforts involving athletics, competition, and victory. It also removes negative energy, protects health, and boosts any work involving love, divination, and wishes.

Chamomile: Known to many as the gambler's herb, luck in games of chance is only one of chamomile's magical facets. It's great for prophetic dreaming and sound sleep, protection, and hex-breaking. Try it, too, for matters of the heart. A little goes a long way when it comes to love and romance. (*Note:* There are two types of chamomile, German chamomile and Roman chamomile. Roman chamomile should not be ingested by pregnant women.)

---

2. Unless otherwise directed, one tablespoon of herb steeped in one cup of boiling water generally makes a good infusion. Strain out plant material before use.

3. Some herbs are poisonous! Before ingesting any herb, please check a reliable herbal and consult with your health-care practitioner to be sure it's safe for human consumption.

4. If you are prone to allergies or have sensitive skin, a patch test is advisable. Just rub a bit of the herb you intend to use on a small area of skin, then wait twenty-four hours to see if there is a reaction.

Cinnamon: Because it vibrates on such a highly spiritual level, this herb is nearly indispensable. It works well for any effort involving prosperity, love, lust, success, physical energy, and divinatory purposes.

Cloves: This herb works beautifully when it comes to relieving depression, grief, and anxiety. It's also an effective medicine magical herb for issues involving lust, love, luck, and money.

Ginger: Try this herb to increase psychic ability, health, personal power, and general success.

Lavender: Used primarily for protection, lavender also works wonders in efforts that deal with easy childbirth, mental and physical healing, peaceful sleep, love, and longevity.

Mugwort: Since smoking this herb or drinking its infusion induces an altered state of consciousness conducive to psychic awareness, mugwort is commonly known as the "Witches herb." The infusion is also used as a magical wash for scrying mirrors, crystal balls, and pendulums. (*Note:* Mugwort should not be ingested by pregnant women.)

Nutmeg: This herb works well in magical efforts where love, money, luck, and health are at issue. (*Note:* Nutmeg is not safe when used internally at more than five grams at a time.)

Sage: Used as a main ingredient in Native American smudge sticks, sage removes negative energy and its residue from areas, buildings, and people, when burned. It also works well for efforts involving good health and fortune, wisdom, long life, and wishes.

Flowers

Flowers have a softer, gentler energy than herbs. But make no mistake: They pack a real wallop when it comes to boosting magic. This is because flowers speak straight to the heart and evoke strong emotional responses from humankind. Since human emotion is the matrix from which all magic flows, it stands to reason that the use of flowers in magical work is very powerful stuff.

In fact, we unwittingly use their magic all the time. They travel to birthdays, christenings, and weddings. They preside over funerals and other transitional events, as well. We send them as tokens of love, friendship, and appreciation. Their magic is simple: It speaks straight to the heart and says what we feel when mere words cannot.

One more thing about flowers. The Universe likes them as much as we do. It doesn't care whether they're dried or fresh or where they come from. They don't have to be delivered by the florist or tied up in pretty ribbons. They can be cut from the yard, picked in the woods, or even plucked from the side of the road and gathered together by a rubber band. Just use whatever you have on hand and know that your message will not only reach the Universe, but ring loud and clear within its Cosmic Ears.

Using flowers in magical work is a snap. Just charge and use them as you would herbs, then try some of the tips that follow. You'll never again think of flowers in the same way.

- Gather several flowers appropriate to your magical intent and wash them thoroughly in cold water. Remove the stems and leaves, then add the petals and buds to a glass of fresh water. Leave the glass overnight under the light of a Waxing or Full Moon, then strain out the flowers. Drink the water to infuse yourself with the magical properties of the flower.[5]

- Write a wish, spell, or incantation on a small piece of paper, then acquire the bud of a flower that's appropriate to your purpose. Place the bud in a vase (don't forget to add water) and put the paper underneath. When the bud blossoms, the magic is done.

- Inscribe a candle with your magical intent, then put it beside a flower bud in a vase. Light the candle and let it burn all the way down. When the bud begins to blossom, so will the magic.

A few easy-to-find flowers and their magical uses are listed for your convenience. For a larger list, check appendix B in the back of this book.

---

5. Some flowers are poisonous! Before ingesting any flower, please check a reliable herbal to be sure it's safe for human consumption.

Chrysanthemum: Because mums contain a natural component called pyrethrum that repels fleas, this flower is often used in efforts involving the protection of animals. Use it, too, for repelling nosy neighbors and unwanted guests. (*Note:* This flower is poisonous when ingested.)

Daisy: This flower promotes joy and makes you feel good all over. It also works wonders when you need to take yourself a little less seriously. (*Note:* This flower is poisonous when ingested.)

Honeysuckle: Usually found growing in the woods or on fences, this fragrant vine relieves stress and lifts the spirits. It also works well when used in efforts involving prosperity, good luck, and an increase in psychic awareness. (*Note:* The berries of this flower could disturb the digestive system if used internally.)

Iris: Sacred to the Goddess of the same name, this flower represents the bridge between life and death. For this reason, it's often used in matters that deal with reincarnation and contacting members of the spirit world. Try it, too, for efforts involving courage and wisdom. (*Note:* Some species of this flower are poisonous when ingested.)

Lilies: Often used in bad habit and hex-breaking efforts, this flower also works wonders when courage, protection, and purification are at issue.

Pansy: The pansy sends a very special message to the Universe. Simply put, the message is "don't forget." For this reason, pansies are often used in efforts involving studies, knowledge retention, clarity of mind, and good memory.

Roses: Renowned for its love-bringing properties, roses also work well in rituals involving fresh starts, luck, protection, prophetic dreaming, and psychic awareness. The green parts of this flower are poisonous. The petals are safe for internal use. (*Note:* The stems and leaves of this flower may be toxic. Do not ingest.)

Sweet Pea: This flower promotes friendship and brings joy to all relationships. It also works well in efforts where getting to the truth of a matter is at issue. (*Note:* This flower is poisonous when ingested.)

Trees

Trees are important in the physical world. We use them to build houses and furniture and fencing. They provide paper and pencils, glue and sealants. But that's not all. Trees also supply the oxygen necessary for normal breathing, and to a large degree, control the moisture in the air. Without them, life as we know it would simply cease to exist.

Trees are also important in the magical world. Their leaves, flowers, roots, and bark often comprise the main ingredients in incenses, oils, powders, and washes. We use them for tool-making and altar construction. Magical symbols are carved on their wood and used for runes and other divinatory devices. Their by-products are tucked into charm bags and send messages to the Universe. The list of magical uses goes on and on.

While all portions of the tree can boost magical work, some parts just work better than others when it comes to specific kinds of magic. The guidelines that follow will help you decide which is best for the effort at hand.

- If it grows below the Earth (roots and root bark), use it for mundane issues like physical and mental stability, grounding, and practicality.

- If it grows on the trunk (bark and moss), try it for efforts involving physical, mental, and emotional health.

- If it grows into the sky (leaves and flowers), it's most effective for issues that deal with freedom, divine guidance or intervention, and planetary work.

As with all other magical boosters, tree properties and energies vary from species to species. Use the following list as a starting point. (For a more extensive list, check appendix B in the back of this book.)

Apple: Sacred to Aphrodite, the Goddess of Love, the gifts of this tree—especially the blossoms—go far in efforts of love, romance, and seduction. The fruit is also used as a symbol of the Craft, for when sliced crosswise, the seeds and core form a perfect pentagram. For this reason, gifts of the apple tree are also used to add power to every type of magic.

Birch: Birch gifts work best in efforts involving new beginnings and fresh starts, but because this tree is sacred to the Earth Mother, it's said that She takes a personal interest in every request made beneath its branches. (For expedient results

45

you must also mention Her name!) Because the birch is also sacred to Thor—and stripping the tree incurs His wrath—take care to harvest its gifts only from a tree that's been struck by lightning, or from twigs and branches scattered on the ground.

Fir: Because this tree is an evergreen, its gifts are frequently used in efforts that deal with immortality and infinity issues, such as reincarnation or karma. They also work well for matters involving good health and physical energy. (*Note:* Some species of fir are poisonous.)

Grapevine: Sacred to Bacchus, the God of Wine, gifts from this vine offer the elements of joy, happiness, and celebration to magical work. Because its fruit is used in wine—and wine alters the state of consciousness—grapevine and its by-products are sometimes used in efforts to promote psychic awareness, as well.

Hawthorn: Commonly burned in ancient Roman temples to clear them of negative energy, hawthorn is often used for cleansing measures. Use the branches as smudge sticks, and the leaves, bark, and thorns to break bad habits. Because the flowers are sacred to the fairies, they work well in issues involving freedom.

Hazel: Long used as divining rods to locate water and minerals, the gifts of this tree work well in efforts involving knowledge retention, wisdom, and cutting through deceit.

Oak: Because the white-berried mistletoe grows among its branches—and the berries represent the semen of the Lord of the Forest—the oak tree is a symbol of strength and masculinity. Use the leaves for health issues, the acorns for prosperity, and the root and bark for mental stability. Tucked into a charm bag and carried, any gift of the oak promotes general good fortune. (*Note:* Please consult your health-care practitioner before ingesting products from this tree.)

Rowan (Mountain Ash): Commonly known as the Tree of Life and Protection, people of ancient times frequently planted the rowan beside homes to repel evil spirits and negativity. Use the leaves and berries in incenses, washes, and oils to increase psychic abilities and divination skills, and keep a few twigs in the house to protect from lightning and storm damage. To promote good health and physical energy, always carry a piece of rowan in your pocket or purse. (*Note:* The fruit of this tree is poisonous.)

Willow: Since the words "willow," "Witch," and "Wicca" are derived from the same linguistic root, and wicker is traditionally constructed of willow, this trees link to the Craft is mundane as well as magical. Because the willow is known as the Tree of Death—and because death is imperative for rebirth—newcomers to the religion often make their wands from its wood. The wood of this tree is sacred to Hecate, and works well in efforts where separation, endings, and new beginnings are at issue. The leaves and bark also work well for healing efforts when added to oils, teas, or incense.

When incorporating tree material into your magical work, always charge it first using the instructions provided in the section on herbs. And don't forget to treat the trees that aid your magic with respect. Leave them a gift in return for their help. It doesn't have to be anything fancy. A few pennies, some cornmeal, or a fertilizer stick or two will do. Remember to treat them as friends, and they'll always supply you with what you need when the time comes.

Stones

Stones, perhaps, influence the human psyche more greatly than any other matter on Earth. Why? For one thing, stones have an inherent power that comes from their ancient existence. They hold the collective consciousness of every ancient culture that ever walked the face of the Earth, and have the ability to impart this knowledge to us. Another reason has to do with their beauty. Because they take shape and grow in every color imaginable, they speak to our emotions. And, of course, this affects us both spiritually and physically.

As important as these things are, though, the main reason we use stones in magical work has very little to with either. To a large degree, stones comprise our Earthly foundation. They provide us with solid ground and support us as we work and play. Because we live on the Earth—and because we are truly the source of all magic—stones form a direct link between the physical and spiritual worlds. Simply put, they stabilize our magic and keep it from flying into the Universe helter-skelter.

Gathering a Stone Supply

Stone collecting used to be expensive for me. That was because I thought that each and every item had to be a flawless, gem-quality piece. And it wasn't until after my wallet was empty and useless that I realized my mistake.

Stones don't have to be faceted works of art to perform effective magic. It doesn't matter whether they cost five thousand dollars per carat or thirty cents per pound. It makes no difference whether they're cut or tumbled. The Universe simply doesn't care. All it's concerned with are the energies that each stone exudes. And all stones—regardless of what they look like—exude the same energy of every other stone in their species.

Another boon to the pocketbook is that magical stone supplies don't have to be large to be powerful. In fact, you can probably get by with less than a handful. The reason for this is that most stones contain multiple properties, and you can use them over and over. Take amethyst, for instance. You can hold it in your hand to relieve stress, then, with a little recharging, tuck it under your pillow to ensure a good night's sleep. It can bring love and harmony, protect you and your property, and bring wisdom, psychic awareness, and good health. Some say it can even relieve drunkenness. The point is, you just don't need ten stones when one will do the trick.

But how do you pick the right stones for your magic? Fact is, you don't. You let the stones pick you. While this may sound ridiculous at first, you have to remember that the Cosmic Plane is built much differently than ours. There's no egotism. No superiority of species. And as such, the same rules just don't apply. It's built on a simple premise and code of ethics. So shake off any preconceived notions, open your mind, and try the selection tips that follow. You'll wind up with the perfect stones for your work. Guaranteed.

1. Begin by closing your eyes and running your dominant hand over a dish of stones.

2. Feel the energy exchange between your hand and the stones. (This will either be a feeling of warmth or a slight tingle.)

3. When several areas feel warmer than others, pick the stones from these areas and set them aside.

4. Repeat the process with the group you set aside until only one stone feels warm.

Cleansing Stones

It's always a good idea to cleanse your stone before charging it for magical use. Why? Because you have no idea where the stone has been or who might have handled it. You don't have a clue as to what it's been used for. And there's no telling what sort of energy it's been exposed to. All of this is important when it comes to magical work. For effectiveness, you need a clean, spiritually unblemished stone that carries no one's vibrations but your own.

Start by washing the stone with soap and cool water. (Use a toothbrush to remove any surface dirt or debris.) Rinse the stone well in clear water while chanting something simple like:

> *Be cleansed of negativity*
> *As I will, so mote it be*

Dry the stone thoroughly with an absorbent cloth or paper towel, then place it in a zippered plastic bag and pop it in the freezer. (If you're cleansing several stones, it's okay to put them in the same bag.) Leave the bag in the freezer for twenty-four hours to clear any previous energies.

Charging Stones

Charging stones is a little different than charging herbs and plants. Not to worry, though. It's just as easy. The instructions below will bring quick and powerful magic to all your stones.

1. Grasp the stone tightly in your dominant hand, and hold it firmly against your third eye.

2. Concentrate on your magical need and visualize it coming to fruition.

3. Chant something appropriate to your need. If charging a rose quartz for self-love, for instance, you might chant something like:

> *Gentle, subtle, pinkest stone*
> *Skills in self-love, help me hone*

Keep chanting until you feel the stone begin to pulse. (This feels a little like a heartbeat, and lets you know that the stone is charged and ready for magical use.)

Basic Stone Supply Guide

While you already know that you don't need a large stone supply for magical work, sometimes it's difficult to decide which stones to acquire. For this reason, a basic stone supply guide follows. (For further information about stones, see appendix C in the back of this book.) The stones listed will serve you well and handle nearly any problems that come your way. Remember, though, this list comprises only the bare basics. You'll want to add to your supply as you work more with the stones and learn more about their world.

Aventurine: This stone works wonders for increasing business and finances. Just carry a charged piece in your purse or pocket.

Amethyst: Great for squelching anger, stress, and depression, amethyst also relieves insomnia, wards off nightmares, and brings prophetic dreams. It also works well in efforts involving love and romance, self-confidence, freedom from addictions, physical and emotional healing, and spiritual guidance.

Apache Tear: Commonly carried for good luck, this stone is also an excellent bet for efforts of protection and divination.

Calcite, Orange: Since this stone amplifies every magical vibration it comes in contact with, it's generally used in combination with other stones. Used alone, it's effective for amplifying emotions.

Citrine: While citrine is commonly used for emotional balance, it's also terrific for promoting inspiration and ideas, artistic endeavors, and any effort where creativity is an issue. It also provides quick relief from nightmares.

Fluorite: Commonly known as the "Student's Stone," fluorite aids mental ability, study, and knowledge retention.

Hematite: If you feel "scattered," this is the stone for you! An excellent grounder, hematite also increases personal magnetism, aids in health issues, and protects physically and emotionally. Because it's also the stone of warriors, use it, too, for courage in the face of animosity.

Opal: This is a very lucky stone when given in love. Commonly known as the "Stone of Karma," opals work well not only to soften karmic retribution, but also help in remembering past lives and lessons learned. Because opals contain all colors of the spectrum, they may be charged for any magical intent.

Quartz, Clear: Clear quartz is the most common stone used in magic today. It may be charged for any magical purpose, or used in combination with other stones to amplify their powers.

Quartz, Rose: Commonly used for efforts of love and romance, rose quartz goes unsurpassed when it comes to promoting self-love. It is also said to clear acne if rubbed on the face.

Quartz, Smoky: This stone promotes both emotional and physical health. Double-terminated pieces also bring balance between the mundane and spiritual worlds.

Sodalite: A very spiritual stone, sodalite stills fear, anxiety, and stress. It also works well when used as a meditational tool to contact spirit guides.

Unakite: Use this stone to see beauty in even the most dismal of circumstances. Try it, too, for uncovering deception and cutting to the truth of the matter.

PART TWO

TOOLS OF
THE TRADE

Magical tools are important, indeed
They bring order and form to the magical need
Attracting, repelling, directing the shape
Flinging open the door and then shutting the gate
On the energy twitching in awesome supply
As it patiently waits for the wherefores and whys
Of the Witch as she lovingly kindles the fire
And stirs up the cauldron of want and desire
But pentacles placed on the altar with pride
And cups, wands, and athames all put aside
The most powerful tool is one often forgot
For it's shelved with the cobwebs and dust and what-not
It sits on our shoulders—it's with us all day
And whether we work or we study or play
It brings all to action and supreme, it does reign:
The most powerful magical tool is the brain!

Dorothy Morrison

MAGICAL TOOLS

Magical tools determine the amount of magical success the practitioner can expect to enjoy.

HAVING THE RIGHT TOOLS[1] for the job is always important, but this is especially true for the Witch. Why? Because the Witch's tools are more than just simple implements to get the job done. They are not only a personal extension of the practitioner, but, to a large degree, determine the amount of magical success the practitioner can expect to enjoy. For these reasons, we usually create our tools from natural materials, or personalize them in such a way that they are unmistakably ours alone.

Since ritual tools are as much a part of the Witch as their arms and legs, we never use or borrow someone else's. In fact, we never so much as touch another person's tools without their permission. To do so is an invasion of privacy. More important, though, one quick touch could imprint the tools with your personal impressions. Left uncleansed, those impressions could involve you karmically in any magical endeavors—positive or negative—in which the tool participates. And that's a place you don't want to go.

---

1. My tradition subscribes to the Element, direction, color, and gender correspondences that I've listed with each tool. You may find that other traditions differ in tool correspondence charts.

THE WAND

Fairy tales and childhood impressions aside, the wand is probably the most important utensil in the Witch's toolbox.

Element: Air

Direction: East

Color: Yellow

Gender: Male/Female

FOLKS THE WORLD OVER associate Witches with magic wands. Perhaps it's because nearly every childhood story written about Witches connects them to the tool. That being the case, the mind's eye views it not only as a symbol of magical power and essence, but as the instrument necessary to manifest any number of supernatural phenomena in the physical realm.

Fairy tales and childhood impressions aside, though, the wand *is* probably the most important utensil in the Witch's toolbox. That's because its magical uses are so widespread. It's an attractant, a repellent, a director of energies. It divides the worlds during Circle-casting, then connects them again when the magic is done. Simply put, it's the one tool that most serious practitioners just can't and won't do without.

What seems most interesting to Craft newcomers, though, is that there's more than just one wand in the Witches' basic tool assortment. Of course, there's the small wand made famous by storytellers. But there's also a larger wand that closely resembles a staff. Both are equally important in magical work, and both can be used to cast Circle. If that's so, then what's the difference? The small wand is generally used to conduct and direct energy. The large wand, however, is better suited toward attracting and repelling energy. It's a little like having two sides of a magical coin. They can either work together or independently of each other to achieve the desired result.

Understanding the Wand and Its Uses

Before we begin to create the wands, it's important to understand exactly what they are, and what they are capable of. A good way to do this is to list all the types of "rods" you can think of, along with their purpose. A partial list is provided below, but don't stop there. Put on your thinking cap and make your own list. Only then will you fully understand what the wand means to you and be able to make the personal connection necessary for successful use.

Wand Chart

Physical Manifestation	Purpose & Capability
Drinking straw	Matter mobilization
Pencil	Communication, definition
Ruler	Measurement, division
Stick or club	Defense, separation
Board	Building
Candle	Illumination
Closet pole	Support

Locating Wand Materials

Since preinitiate wands are traditionally created from the wood of a living fruit or willow tree, making these tools takes some time. It isn't as simple as cutting a couple of branches. You must first find a tree that appears to be healthy and strong. And then you have to befriend it. This isn't always as easy as it sounds. Fact is, you have to talk to it. Get to know it. Hug it and love it. You even have to bring it gifts. (Cornmeal, tobacco, and fertilizer sticks are good choices.) Yes, this sort of behavior tends to raise the eyebrows of unsuspecting passersby. For this reason, you may wish to work with a tree in the privacy of your back yard, or locate one in a fairly remote area.

Once you've formed a good rapport with the tree, ask permission to cut its branches. Tell it that you will need a small branch and a large one for your magical work. Put your arms around it and listen for its response. You may not actually hear it speaking at this point, but should get a feeling of how to proceed. If the response is negative or you get no feeling at all, don't worry. Know that the tree has its own reasons for denying your request. (Even though it's not apparent, the tree could be sick or too weak to accommodate you.) Just go on to another tree, form a new friendship, and try again. Eventually, you'll find the tree that's right for you.

If the response is of a positive nature, however, thank the tree by giving it a hug. Then, walking in a counterclockwise direction, encircle its base while visualizing a protective circle of white light forming around it. Feed the tree positive energy, and leave it a small gift before saying goodbye.

Wand Harvest

Continue to visit the tree, but wait until the next Full Moon to harvest the necessary branches. The small wand should measure the distance from the tip of your middle finger to your elbow, and the diameter should be no larger than the widest part of your thumb. The large wand should be thirty-nine inches long and no larger than two inches in diameter. Because you'll want to cause your friend the least amount of discomfort possible, pay careful attention to the harvest instructions outlined on the following page. And once the process is finished, remember to continue your visits with the tree. It will not only be a friend for life, but a source of personal power in your magical life.

Materials

	Yardstick or tape measure
	Pencil or marking pen
2	12-inch lengths of ribbon or cord
	Sharp handsaw
5–6	Fertilizer sticks (gift for the tree)

Gather the materials and locate the tree. Talk to it a bit. Hug it, stroke it, and remind it of the reason for your visit.

Measure the appropriate branch lengths and clearly mark the cutting lines, then tie a piece of ribbon tightly around each limb about a foot closer to the trunk than the cutting mark. Using the side of the handsaw, tap the end of the first branch three times and say:

> *Spirit of this Tree, my Friend*
> *To lower portions now descend*
> *Until I've done what I must do*
> *So no harm or damage comes to You*

Repeat with the second limb, then make the cuts quickly and smoothly.
Untie the ribbons and give the tree a big hug. Call its spirit back by saying:

> *O Spirit of this Tree, my Friend*
> *From trunk and root depths now ascend*
> *Into the form You've always been*
> *Grow tall, be well, and green again*

Shove the fertilizer sticks into the ground at the base of the trunk, thank the tree, and leave.

Wand Creation

Now that you have the wand material, it's time to get on with the fun stuff! And though toolmaking is undoubtedly serious business, it's important to unleash your creativity and enjoy the process. It's also important not to get in a hurry. The more time you spend working on your tools, the more energy you put into them. And it's your personal energy that makes them powerful. Besides, you have plenty of time to prepare and decorate your wands exactly as you want. You won't be consecrating them until the light of the next Full Moon, at the earliest.

Materials

 Fine grain sandpaper
 Sharp knife
 Clean, soft paintbrush
3 tablespoons dried chamomile
 Almond oil or a floral/fruity essential oil of your choice
 Paper towels
 Stones, feathers, seashells, and so on (optional)
 Wood glue or rubber cement (optional)

Remove all small branches and bark from the wands. (If the bark doesn't strip away easily, try soaking the rods in the bathtub overnight to loosen it.) Then smooth the wands with sandpaper.

Using the knife, carefully carve a notch in the large wand ends, and whittle the small ends into points. (These shapes symbolize the female and male energies, respectively.) Sand both ends until smooth.

Carve runes or symbols into them, or add your name if you like. (For ideas, see the charts at the end of this section.)

Add three tablespoons of dried chamomile to a cup of boiling water, cover, and allow to steep for thirty minutes. (If you can't find dried chamomile, don't fret. Just pick up a box of Celestial Blends Sleepy-Time Tea at the supermarket. It's made of chamomile and will work just as well. Use three teabags to one cup of water.) As the tea steeps, enchant it by saying something like:

> *Herb of great power—of magic and grace—*
> *Flow into this liquid, and now interlace*
> *Your strength and your might as you steep into tea*
> *In the names of the Ancient Ones, so mote it be*

After the tea cools, use the paintbrush to completely cover both wands five times with the solution. As you cover the wands, chant:

Wand, gather the magic from this herbal soak
Grow in power and might with my every stroke

Allow the wands to air dry in a dark place for three days.

Rub a generous amount of almond or essential oil between your hands, then work the oil into the wands to prevent the wood from cracking. Allow them to rest for the next three days.

If you like, decorate the wands with stones, shells, feathers, or other items. Use whatever materials you want. If you'd prefer plain, undecorated wands, that's okay, too. The idea here is to personalize the wands and make them distinctly yours.

Blessing Ritual

Materials

> White candle
> Sandalwood incense
> Small dish of water
> Salt

Set aside some time on the night of the next Full Moon to bless the wands. Sitting comfortably on the floor with the materials and wands in front of you, light the candle and incense. Breathe in deeply through your nose while visualizing the grounding energy of the Earth filling your body. Then exhale fully through your mouth, expelling all negative energy. Repeat this process until you feel completely at ease and relaxed.

Pass the wands through the incense smoke and say:

> *With scented Air so light and free*
> *I give you breath now. Blessed be!*

Being careful not to burn yourself or catch the wands on fire, pass them quickly through the candle flame and say:

> *With Fire that dances wild and free*
> *I give you passion. Blessed be!*

Lightly sprinkle the wands with water and say:

> *With Water so pure, I give to Thee*
> *The blood of Life now. Blessed be!*

Sprinkle the wands with a bit of salt and say:

> *With the salt of the Earth, I give to Thee*
> *Roots in magic. Blessed be!*

Then hold the wands close to your heart and lovingly caress them with your fingers. Say:

> *I am yours and you are mine*
> *From now until the end of time*
> *I give you Life now willingly*
> *As I will, so mote it be!*

Tool Consecration Ritual

After the wands are blessed, it's time to consecrate them. Take the wands outdoors if possible, and hold them up to the Moon. Then invoke the Lord and Lady by saying something like:

> *Lord and Lady, hear my plea*
> *Please be present here with me*
> *As I dedicate these wands to You*
> *And to Your work—both old and new*
> *Lend Your power and Your might*
> *Infuse them with Your love and light*
> *Bless these wands I offer Thee*
> *As I will, so mote it be*

The wands are now ready for magical use. Wrap the wands in cloth as an insulative measure against the vibrations of others, and store them away until you're ready to use them.

Magical Theory: Large Wand Exercises
(Week One)

Exercise One: Attracting

Grasp the large wand with your left hand. With thumb and index finger facing away from you, place the notched end against the middle of your torso (just beneath your ribcage). With thumb and index finger facing away from you, grip the middle of the wand with your right hand while pointing it about three to four inches from the wall. (*Note:* Reverse these instructions if you are left-handed.) Close your eyes and visualize the wand pulling you toward the wall. Within a matter of seconds, the small wand end will settle against the wall.

Perform this exercise five to ten times each day for a week. Record your progress.

Exercise Two: Repelling

Standing with a chair behind you, hold the wand as described in Exercise One. Close your eyes and visualize the wand thrusting you away from the wall. You will quickly lose your balance and fall into the chair.

Perform this exercise five to ten times each day for a week. Record your progress.

Astral Wand Exercises
(Week Two)

Exercise Three: Wand Visualization

Wrap and store the wand. Repeat Exercises One and Two while visualizing the wand in your hand.

Perform this exercise five to ten times each day for a week. Record your progress.

Exercise Four: Attracting and Repelling People and Places

Repeat Exercise Three, but instead of using the wall as the object of the exercise, work with attracting and repelling a person or place. (This is also a great exercise for attracting what you want from life, and clearing out any negative energy.)

Perform this exercise five to ten times each day for a week. Record your progress.

Small Wand Exercises
(Weeks Three and Four)

Exercise Five: Circling and Directing

Place a cup, bud vase, figurine, or other object on a table or windowsill in your room. Using the pointed tip of the small wand, draw a circle around the object in a clockwise motion. Point the wand at the object, and close your eyes. Concentrate on a musical note, a simple song, or a nursery rhyme. Then direct that energy from your mind and will it to travel down your shoulder and arm, wrist and hand. Will it to travel down the length of the wand, out through its tip, and into the object.

Continue to work with this exercise daily, building the power and infusing the object until it is completely saturated.

The goal is to eventually hear the sound when you enter the room. Record your progress.

Exercise Six: Circling and Rejecting

Bring something into your room that doesn't belong there. Put it in a prominent place—a place where you'll see it every day. (It doesn't matter what the object is. It could be a bar of soap, a can of green beans, or even a roll of toilet paper. Just make sure that it's something that would not normally be in your room.) Using the pointed end of the wand, draw a circle around it in a counterclockwise motion. Then point the wand at the object, close your eyes, and, using the same energy flow technique in Exercise Five, will it to be gone. Try to ignore the object unless you're working with this exercise.

Continue to work with this exercise daily, building the power to reject the object. The goal is to be able to come and go in the room without noticing the object. Record your progress.

Witches or Theban Alphabet

A	ᚱ
B	ᚴ
C	ᛘ
D	ᛘ
E	ᚱ
F	ᛂ
G	ᚢ
H	ᛉ
I	ᚢ
J	ᚼ
K	ᛢ
L	ᚤ
M	ᚵ
N	ᛁ
O	ᛘ
P	ᛂ
Q	ᚱ
R	ᛘ
S	ᚸ
T	ᚵ
U	ᚱ
V	ᚱ
W	ᚱ
X	ᚢ
Y	ᚴ
Z	ᛘ

Futhark Runes

ᚠ	Success
ᚻ	Growth, change
ᚦ	Defense
ᚨ	Communication
ᚱ	Travel
ᚲ	Creativity
ᚷ	Union
ᚹ	Wishes granted
ᚾ	Chaos
ᛁ	Stability
ᛁ	Checkmate
ᛃ	Gifts
ᛇ	Transition
ᛈ	Quest, discovery
ᛉ	Protection
ᛋ	Victory
↑	Commitment
ᛒ	Birth
ᛗ	Flexibility
ᛘ	Relationships
ᛚ	Intuition, magic
ᛝ	Transformation
ᛟ	Emergence
ᛜ	Ancestors, past lives

Magical Symbols

The Lady

The Lord

Triple Goddess

Triple God

Air

Fire

Water

Earth

Karmic Law

THE CUP

Practitioners the world over have been using silver cups since the birth of the Craft—not because of their ascetic beauty, but because they work!

Element: Water

Direction: West

Color: Blue

Gender: Female

WHILE THE WAND MOVES and directs energy, the ritual cup or chalice performs tasks of a completely different variety. First, we use it in ritual Circle as a drinking device during both personal and Deity libations. But the cup is much more than that. It also acts as a magical containment area for any substance—mundane, psychic, or otherwise—that the practitioner deems necessary, and keeps it there until the time comes to release it. Simply put, the cup's purpose is to gather, hold, and disperse energy.

The ritual cup is traditionally cast of sterling silver, the metal of the Moon. That's because its ruling element is Water, and the rise and ebb of the ocean tides are ruled by the Moon. The two walk hand in hand. Since sterling silver can be exorbitantly expensive, however, most practitioners opt for silver plate or some other silver-colored metal.

What if silver doesn't trip your trigger, though? What if pottery is more your style? Or, for that matter, Waterford crystal? While I've seen practitioners use other types of cups, beginners seem to have better luck with silver ones. For one thing, it provides the proper tool/Moon/Element symbology and puts you in the right frame of mind. For another, the inner surface of a silver-colored goblet is more conducive to collecting the types of intangible matter necessary to the exercises than any other surface. Most important, though, is that practitioners the world over have been using silver cups since the birth of the Craft—not because of their ascetic beauty, but because they work!

Obtaining the Cup

Unless you're an experienced metalsmith, creating your own ritual cup isn't an option. But then what do you do? How do you find the one that's exactly right for you?

You simply ask the deities for help. You don't need to perform a fancy ritual; in fact, no ritual is necessary at all. Just explain your plight and ask Them to guide you in the search.

Then do some legwork. Visit local New Age shops. Try area thrift stores, consignment, and antique shops. Check the newspaper for estate auction sales. Don't discount yard sales or flea markets, either. Some of my most powerful tools were once someone else's castoffs!

What if you try all that and still come up short? Don't fret. Don't get in a hurry. Resist the urge to buy something just to make do. Understand that *your* ritual cup just hasn't been made available yet, and resolve to wait until it has. This isn't a foot race, after all. It's a search for a magical tool. And sometimes the search, itself, is just as important to personal growth as the end result. You never know who you might meet or what you might learn on the way. Just relax and keep looking. The right cup will eventually cross your path—and when it does, you'll know beyond the shadow of a doubt that it belongs to you.

Purchasing Tools

You've found the perfect tool. You know that it's yours. You can even see yourself using it in magic more powerful than any other on the planet. Then you turn it over to check the price. Your face falls. All happy visions fade from the mind's eye.

There's no way you can afford it. And yet, you just know that the two of you belong together. What then?

First things first: No matter how badly you want it, don't even think of haggling over the price. Doing so not only cheapens the Craft, but lessens the magic of the tool. Either way, it's a no-win situation.

Instead, get a firm grasp of the situation and explore your options. Check to see if the store offers layaway or some sort of purchase plan. Failing that, there may be other options. Small store owners (Pagan ones, in particular) will occasionally take barter in exchange for merchandise. If you're not comfortable with that, then ask if they need any help in the store. You might wind up with a part-time job, an employee discount, and the cup of your dreams to boot! (Remember, if it's meant to be, the Universe will come to your aid. All you have to do is ask.)

Understanding the Cup and Its Uses

Before working with the cup, it's a good idea to completely understand its importance, its uses, and what to expect from it magically. A good way to do this is to make two lists. First, write down all the types of "cups" you can think of. Then make another list to define the uses of a cup's contents. For your convenience, I have provided a partial list for you. This is only a starting point, though. Make your own lists in your personal notebook or journal.

Cup Charts
A cup can be:

Human body	Ocean	The mind
Ditch	Seashell	Lake
Cave	Hand	Tomb

A cup's contents can:

Be emptied	Bring joy	Poison
Feed and nurture	Cleanse	Become stagnant
Intoxicate	Refresh	Warm or chill

Cup Consecration

On the night of the next Full Moon, wash your cup with warm, soapy water, and rinse it well. Visualize any negative energy being sucked down the drain with the rinse water. Dry the tool thoroughly, and give it a good polishing. Then perform the Blessing Ritual described in the section titled Wands.

After the Blessing Ritual, take the cup outside to a brook, river, stream, fountain, or some other body of running water. (If this isn't possible, work at the kitchen or bathroom sink instead.) Rinse the cup well in cold, running water, and hold it up to the sky. Say:

Gracious Goddess of the Moon
Whose blood is mine and flows in tune
With the pulse of Nature and its dance
I offer You this tool; enhance
Its magical success
And with Your gentle hand, please bless
Its work with laughter and with love
O Goddess of the Moon above
So that it serves both Thee and me
As I will, so mote it be

The cup is now ready for magical use. Wrap it in a soft cloth and keep it stored away when you're not using it.

Magical Theory: Moonlight Cup Exercises (Weeks One Through Three)

Exercise One: Filling

Take the cup outdoors on a moonlit night. Hold the cup so it fills with the light. Watch carefully as the moonlight moves and pulses in the cup as if it's a living, breathing entity. Dip your finger into the light and try to make it dance up your finger.

Repeat this exercise every night for one week, and record your progress.

Exercise Two: Emptying

Take the cup outdoors on a moonlit night. Hold the cup as in Exercise One until it fills with living moonlight. Then try to pour out the light.

Repeat this exercise every night for one week, and record your progress.

Exercise Three: Singing Down the Moon (Scrying)

Fill the cup with cold water, then take it outside on a moonlit night. Sit comfortably on the ground and sing or hum "Greensleeves." (If you don't know this song, try another slow, romantic tune.) As you sing, focus on the Moon's reflection on the water. Watch carefully as other images appear.

Repeat this exercise every night for one week, and record your progress.

Magical Theory: Indoor Cup Exercise (Weeks Four Through Six)

Exercise Four: Wish Magic

Write a wish on a piece of paper. Keep it simple and reasonable. (Wishing for a million dollars to materialize probably won't bring expedient results!) It's also important to put forth any personal effort necessary to aid in successful wish manifestation. (After all, you're not likely to get the job you want without applying for it or at least sending a resume.) Fold the paper in half and place it in the cup.

Visualizing every detail in vivid color, see the wish coming true. Then run your index finger around the rim of the cup in a clockwise motion while chanting:

By the Ancient Ones and Cosmic Divine
What I wish for now be mine
Bring it to me quick and fast
As I will, this spell is cast

Repeat the visualization and chant every day for the duration of this exercise. When the wish comes true, tear the paper into tiny pieces and flush it down the toilet. (If the wish manifests before the end of the three-week period, begin the exercise again with a new wish.) Record your progress.

THE ATHAME

The athame works much like a magical cafeteria supervisor, ensuring that everything runs smoothly and that no one spoils the soup.

Element: Fire

Direction: South

Color: Red

Gender: Male

ALTHOUGH THE WAND AND athame [a'-tha-may *or* a-thaw'-may] are sometimes used interchangeably for casting Circle, the two have very different purposes. Instead of moving and directing energy, the athame invokes and banishes it. It also tends to unseen entities and forces. This is important because it holds negative spirits at bay and keeps them from wreaking havoc with spellwork, while attracting and inviting those entities who possess vibrations that are beneficial to the tasks at hand. In short, the athame works much like a magical cafeteria supervisor, ensuring that everything runs smoothly and that no one spoils the soup.

Traditionally, the athame is a double-edged blade with a black handle. Why black? Because black is the absence of color rather than a color in itself. This means that it's capable of grabbing negative forces and digesting them. Once digested and stripped of their power, it then transforms these forces into a harmless energy that dissipates quickly and easily into the Universe. The athame is a wonderful tool that few Witches are willing to do without.

The double-edged blade is an entirely different story, though. First, it reminds us that there are two sides to the magical coin: Life (positive) and Death (negative). And since we are the masters of our own destinies, it's up to us to choose which side of the coin we will play. We can either use our magic to defend and protect and work toward the good of all, or we can place our bets on the dark side and cut our own throats. The choice is up to us.

The blade, itself, is usually made of steel. There really isn't a magical reason for this, but it's important just the same. Here's why: The athame blade must be heated to very high temperatures during the consecration ceremony, and most other metals just won't stand up to it. So, unless you're willing to take a chance on melting your athame and having to start over, steel is truly the best bet.

Just a couple more things about the athame. First, it should *never* be used to draw blood. If it is, the tool must be destroyed in such a way that it can never be used again. That having been said, please be careful when working with this tool. It would be a pity to spend all that time searching for the perfect blade, only to have it rendered useless by one careless slip of the finger!

Second, and just as important, please check with your local law enforcement agency before taking your athame out in public. Why? Because in some areas of the country, a blade of any sort is categorized as a "weapon," and public display of a weapon is unlawful; arguing with the police that the athame is a "ritual tool" just isn't going to cut it. Know your city, county, and state ordinances, and you'll go a long way toward steering clear of unnecessary trouble.

Now, let's get started!

Obtaining the Athame

While you can order your athame from any number of reputable cutlery companies, they're usually relatively expensive. I discovered a great alternative during my search, though. Believe it or not, it was the local pawn shop! The selection was as good or better than those found in most of the cutlery catalogues, and they even had some really obscure specialty blades. Not only was it an athame-hunter's dream-come-true, the prices were great, too!

When obtaining your athame, please follow the same guidelines set forth for obtaining the cup. Remember to keep searching until you find the one that's exactly right for you, and above all—don't haggle over the price.

Athame Consecration

Unlike most of the other tool consecrations, the one for the athame is performed during the Waning Moon. It's also lengthy and could take several days or several weeks to complete. Remember that there's no need to hurry. Take your time. Do it right. The results? A wonderful tool whose magic you can always depend on.

Materials

3   cups boiling water
1   teaspoon each of five of the following: chili powder,
      chrysanthemum, Dragon's blood, hellebore,
      henbane, pansies, poppy seed, rue, sulphur (the scrapings
      of five match heads may be substituted for sulphur
      if you like)
3   drops of your blood*
    Wooden spoon
    Campfire with hot coals (a charcoal fire in a barbecue grill
      also works well)
    Oven mitt
    Incense (your choice)
    Small dish of water
    Lodestone or magnet

(* Please *do not* use a straight pin or a knife for this! Such items are unsanitary and you could wind up with a serious infection. Use a lancet instead. They're inexpensive and readily available in your local pharmacy.)

During the Waning Moon, boil three cups of water and remove from heat. Add five herbs from the list along with three drops of your blood, then stir well. Cover the pot and set aside to cool.

Prepare the camp or grill fire and light it. When the coals are red hot, light the incense. Pass the athame through the smoke and say:

By power of Air so light and free
I cleanse You of all negativity

Sprinkle the athame with water and say:

By power of Water so clear and pure
I cleanse you of energies old and obscure

Holding the athame handle with the oven mitt, heat the blade until it is red hot, saying:

By power of Fire, be cleansed and free
Of your previous life of mundanity

Then plunge the blade into the herbal infusion three times[1], saying with each:

Tool of steel, Your orders be
To banish all things I ask of Thee

Toss the herbal infusion on the fire, then dowse it thoroughly with water. When the fire is extinguished, sit comfortably with the athame and the lodestone or magnet. Stroke both sides of the blade to magnetize it while saying:

Tool of steel, Your orders be
To invoke all things I ask of Thee

Continue the process until the athame easily picks up nails, straight pins, or paper clips. (This may take some time. Work with it for at least an hour to start, then see how the blade reacts to small metal objects. If it doesn't pick them up with ease, continue to work with it at one-hour intervals until it accomplishes the task to your satisfaction.)

---

1. Plunging a hot blade into liquid removes all tempering and tends to pit the metal. Don't worry if this happens to your athame. It doesn't mean that you've done anything wrong, and won't hamper the magic of the tool.

When the blade is magnetized, think about how you'd like to decorate it. Some folks like to carve or paint runes in the handle. Others prefer to tie ribbons, shells, or stones at the hilt. If carving or painting is your thing, do it now. If not, wait until after the next step to adorn the blade.

When you are satisfied with the rune inscriptions, dig a hole in the ground deep enough to completely bury the athame point down. As you cover the tool with Earth, say:

> *I ground You now with the power of Earth*
> *Absorb its stability, its richness and mirth*

Leave the athame in the ground for seventy-two hours, then dig it up. Clean the athame thoroughly with soap and water, and dry it well. Finish decorating the tool, then wrap it in a cloth or sheath until you're ready to use it.

Understanding the Athame and Its Uses

Because the athame is a tool that handles both attraction and banishment—tasks in direct conflict with each other—it's easier to understand its function when thinking in terms of opposites. For that reason, make a list of all the opposites that come to mind. Even though this exercise may seem easy, please don't discount its importance. The more thought you put into this, the better you'll understand the athame and the more magic it will hold for you.

Opposites List

Active	Passive
Light	Dark
Male	Female
Hard	Soft
Sweet	Sour
Wet	Dry
Hot	Cold
Positive	Negative

Once you've completed the opposites list, jot down all the knifelike things that come to mind. Then follow through by listing the purpose and capability of each.

This will not only give you a better idea of what you can expect magically from the athame, but how you can use it to your best advantage.

Athame Chart

Physical Manifestation	Purpose & Capability
Tongue	Attract or repel verbally
Straight edge	Draw a line or boundary
Sword	Protect and defend
Scissors	Cut, trim, shape
Knife	Stab, slice, separate
Razor blade	Scrape, shave, remove
Ice pick	Puncture

Magical Theory: Athame Exercise
(Week One)

Exercise One: Invoking and Banishing Pentagrams

Using the athame and standing at each of the Watchtower directions—East, South, West, and North—practice drawing invoking and banishing pentagrams in the air. (If you're not sure of the directions, please use a compass. It's important that you are standing at the proper place because you will eventually be performing this exercise while calling the Watchtower Guardians during Circle.)

	Invoking			Banishing	
	1			1	
4		3	3		4
2		5	5		2

Repeat this exercise four to five times daily for one week, and record your progress.

Magical Theory: Athame Exercise
(Week Two)

Exercise Two: Inviting

Stand in a doorway while gripping the athame handle in both hands. Point the blade away from you and say:

I invite you in—please come and play
You may go when you wish—but are welcome to stay

Take a step back and move the blade in a vertical motion until it rests point-up on your right shoulder. Close your eyes, clear your mind, and see who comes in.

Repeat this exercise several times daily for one week, and record your progress.

Magical Theory: Athame Exercise
(Week Three)

Exercise Three: Preventing and Dismissing

Holding the athame handle firmly in both hands, stand in a doorway with the point down. Quickly move the blade up until your arms are stretched out in front of you and the blade point faces the doorway. Say fiercely:

You are not welcome—you must leave now. Go!
You must retreat, for I deem it so

Repeat this exercise several times daily for one week, and record your progress.

Magical Theory: Athame Exercise
(Weeks Four and Five)

Exercise Four: Attraction Magic

Think of one positive quality that you'd like to develop in your set of personal characteristics. Name a paper clip for the attribute, then pass the athame over the clip so that it adheres to the blade. While visualizing yourself in possession of that characteristic, say:

Attract this quality to me
As I will so mote it be

Repeat the visualization and chant daily and record your progress. When the attribute is yours, put the paper clip on your key ring and carry it with you.

Magical Theory: Athame Exercise (Weeks Six and Seven)

Exercise Five: Expulsion Magic

Think of one bad habit that you'd like to break. Name a paper clip for the habit and hold it in your dominant hand. Pass the athame over the clip so that it adheres to the blade while visualizing the habit being removed. Say:

Exorcise this trait from me
As I will so mote it be

Repeat the visualization and chant daily and record your progress. When the habit is broken, bury the paper clip where no one will find it.

THE PENTACLE

Worn by Wiccans as a symbol of their craft, pentacles are frequently seen in tarot decks in the form of a card suit. They symbolize the Earth, and its bountiful richness and abundance.

Element: Earth

Direction: North

Color: Green

Gender: Male/Female

ALTHOUGH SOME RITUAL TOOLS seem to hold qualities similar to each other, the pentacle is truly a stand-alone sort of instrument. While its basic function is to shield and protect, it goes one step further. It grounds all energies that we invite and direct, wraps them up into a nice, neat little package, and keeps them from scattering aimlessly through the Universe. In short, the pentacle works as a manifestation device.

There are two types of pentacles: the working pentacle and the ritual pentacle. The working pentacle is a circular piece of wood or paper that is white on one side and black on the other. We use it to give magical energies the form and shape necessary to manifest in the physical world and become reality.

Placed on the altar during Circle, the ritual pentacle is a circular tool with a pentagram at its center. And because of its connection with the Earth, it's usually fashioned of clay, wood, stone, cork, metal, or some other Earth-based product. It holds cakes and wine for blessing during ritual, as well as any magical petitions or requests that we desire to manifest during a working Circle.

The Pentacle Versus the Pentagram

Over the years, I've noticed that a lot of people seem to use these terms interchangeably. It's a mistake, but one that's easy to make. The pentagram is a five-pointed star with a five-sided geometrical shape in its center. The pentacle, on the other hand, is a pentagram or star encapsulated by a circle.

Worn by Wiccans as a symbol of their craft, pentacles are frequently seen in tarot decks in the form of a card suit. They symbolize the Earth, and its bountiful richness and abundance. Within the realm of the tarot, they also represent something we all wish we had more of: money. If you look closely, though, you'll find it in other places, too. For example, have you ever noticed that the bright red Texaco star isn't really a star at all? It's a pentacle, instead.

Used much differently, the pentagram is probably the most maligned symbol on the face of the Earth. In fact, it carries such an impact on society that the advertising media likes to use it to denote evil. They slap it on everything from album covers to theater posters. It's their way of telling us that the entertainment they're selling is so deliciously horrifying that it's guaranteed to scare the daylights out of us.

They're misinformed. And if we buy into that, we are, too.

Drawn with one point up, the pentagram has many meanings. It can represent mind over matter, with the upper point symbolizing the practitioner and the other four, the Elements. It can symbolize the macrocosm of man, for when we stand with our arms and legs outstretched, we, too, form a starlike shape. In the early days of Christianity, it was used to represent the five wounds of Christ. The list goes on and on.

Although sometimes used by Witches to represent the face of the Horned God, the symbol drawn with two points up is more frequently used by Satanists as a symbol of their religion. In this form, it symbolizes matter, or basal instinct over mind. Because I believe that we draw power from the symbols with which we associate ourselves, I never use the pentagram in this form. Please don't misunderstand, though. It's not because I think it's evil. It's simply that I'd rather go through life in full command of the Elements—and of anything else that crosses my path—than to live my life like an ostrich with her head stuck in the sand. I think you get the idea.

Understanding the Pentacle and Its Uses

As with the other tools, you'll better understand the pentacle and its uses by drawing up physical manifestation and purpose and capability lists. Just jot down all of the shieldlike things that come to mind, and follow through with its purpose. The list below will get you started.

Pentacle Chart

Physical Manifestation	Purpose & Capability
Mask	To cover, protect, or hide
Computer monitor	Brings remote data into vision
Jar lid	Protects and preserves
Artist's canvas	Brings ideas into visual reality
Television screen	Relays news and entertainment
Pool	Reflects reality
Potter's wheel	Forms, shapes, and manifests

Making the Ritual Pentacle

Types of ritual pentacles vary from practitioner to practitioner. Some folks like silver or copper and have theirs commissioned to a metalsmith. Others use wood and burn the pentagram into the center, or fashion theirs from ceramic. The possibilities are as endless as the practitioner's imagination. In fact, one of my first ritual pentacles was a round piece of cork with a starfish in the center.

If you know exactly what you want, go for it. If not, try the instructions that follow. The ritual pentacle is not only quick and easy to make, but will serve you well in your ritual endeavors.

Materials

3   packages bakeable clay (available at arts and crafts stores)
    6-inch circular piece of wood or cork
3–4 tablespoons dried, crushed sage or lavender
    Cookie sheet
    Hot glue sticks and hot glue gun

Thoroughly mix the herbs and clay with your fingers while chanting:

Herb of protection, meld with clay
Combine your strengths as one today
Become the power of the Earth
With solid base and joyful mirth

Divide the clay into five equal portions, then rub them between your palms to form long rolls. Place them on the wood or cork to form a five-pointed star, trim if necessary, and join and smooth the ends together. Carefully remove the star and place it on the cookie sheet while chanting:

Star of herb and Earthly might
Bring manifestation into sight
Though magic flows around about
Bring it to reality within and out

Bake according to package directions and allow to cool. Then hot glue it to the wood or cork.

Bless and consecrate the pentacle using the Blessing Ritual and Tool Consecration found in the section titled Wands.

Making the Working Pentacle

Although this pentacle may be constructed of wood, I find it easier—and much less expensive—to make it from poster board. It should be at least twelve inches in diameter for easy use. Use the following instructions, and you'll have a good, serviceable pentacle that works well for the exercises that follow.

Materials

Length of string or twine a couple of inches longer
than the diameter of desired pentacle size
Pencil
1 large sheet white poster board
1 large sheet black poster board
Scissors
White glue

Tie one end of the string around the pencil, then tie a loop in the other end. With your finger in the loop, move the pencil away from you until the string is taut. Positioning your finger in the center of one piece of poster board, use the pencil to draw a circle. Repeat the process for the other piece of poster board, then cut out both circles. Glue the circles together back to back so one side is white and the other is black.

Consecrate the pentacle using the Tool Consecration found in the section about Wands.

Magical Theory: Pentacle Exercise (Weeks One and Two)

Exercise One: Symbol Formation

Gather together a candle, your cup, and your athame, then place the working pentacle, black side out, against the wall at eye level.

Light the candle and turn off the lights. Visualize the cup being filled with a pure white fluid light, then dip the point of the athame into the liquid. Using the athame as a writing tool, draw a pentagram on the pentacle. See the glowing lines of the shape. As the lines dim, dip the athame back into the cup and paint the shape again. The goal is to have the shape remain without need of repainting.

When you are done, erase the shield by passing your hand over the pentacle.

Repeat this exercise nightly for two weeks and record your progress.

Magical Theory: Pentacle Exercise (Weeks Three and Four)

Exercise Two: Word Formation

Repeat Exercise One, but instead of using the athame to draw a pentagram, use it to write words. Start with only one word. When it remains on the pentacle without having to repaint, add another word. Continue to add words until a complete sentence remains. Erase with your hand when finished.

Repeat this exercise nightly for two weeks and record your progress.

Magical Theory: Pentacle Exercise (Weeks Five and Six)

Exercise Three: Picture Formation

Repeat Exercise Two, but instead of using the athame to write sentences, draw a simple picture scene. Don't worry if you're not artistic. Simple stick figures will do. Repaint as necessary. The goal is to have the scene remain on the pentacle without adding more paint. Erase with your hand when finished.

Repeat this exercise nightly for two weeks and record your progress.

Magical Theory: Pentacle Exercise (Week Seven)

Exercise Four: White Shield Work

Repeat Exercises One through Three, but this time work with the white side of the pentacle and visualize the liquid in the cup as being black ink. Erase with your hand when finished.

Work with these exercises nightly for two weeks and record your progress.

Magical Theory: Pentacle Exercise
(Weeks Eight and Nine)

Exercise Five: Scene Projection

With the room darkened and a lit candle placed behind you, sit within reading distance from the black side of the pentacle. Visualize a beam of light streaming from the spot between your eyebrows and onto the pentacle surface. See that light projecting full color images on the surface. Start with simple stationary objects like a bird or a stop sign, for example, and work up to moving scenes with three-dimensional objects and people. Erase with your athame.

Repeat this exercise nightly for two weeks and record your progress.

Magical Theory: Pentacle Exercise
(Weeks Ten and Eleven)

Exercise Six: Scrying and Divination

Repeat Exercise Five, but instead of projecting chosen images, allow the images to come of their own accord. Don't worry if the pentacle fills with mist, then darkens and brightens before anything else happens. This is normal. Try to remember the images so you can record them in your progress notes.

Repeat this exercise nightly for two weeks and record your progress.

OTHER TOOLS AND RITUAL ACCOUTREMENTS

If adding to your repertoire appeals to you, the cauldron, besom, black mirror, and white-handled knife supplement the basic tools.

ALTHOUGH THE WAND, CUP, ATHAME, and pentacle are the four primary tools used in ritual, practitioners often use other ritual items as well. And regardless of what other folks may say, you can perform successful magic with the tools you already have. But if adding to your repertoire appeals to you, read on. A brief description of each tool, related blessing or consecration changes, and necessary exercises follow.

The Cauldron

The cauldron represents Akasha—the mover and shaker of the Elements. It also symbolizes the point of metamorphosis or transformation that occurs during the magical process. And when used in ritual, it is placed at the center of the Circle. The reason for this is that the cauldron is also known as the "Womb of the Goddess" (the source from which all magic flows), and all magic flows from the Circle's center.

In ancient times the cauldron held fire, so the tool was traditionally constructed of cast iron. In this day and time, though, the fire it contains usually takes the form of incense, candles, or paper requests burned on smoldering herbs, so nearly any metal will do.

When obtaining your cauldron, please use the same guidelines as for the cup. Then on the night of the next Dark Moon, wash the cauldron with hot, soapy water. Rinse it well, visualizing any negative energy being sucked down the drain with the rinse water. Dry the cauldron thoroughly, then spritz the inside with a light coating of cooking oil. Wipe any residue away with a paper towel, then perform the Blessing Ritual described in the section on Wands.

Cauldron Consecration

After the Blessing Ritual, take the cauldron outside and sit comfortably beside it. Light a charcoal block, place it in the cauldron, and scatter a little sage on top. (This doesn't have to be any special sort of sage. The kind from the grocery store works fine.) Watch the smoke curl up to the sky. Open your arms to the sky and say:

> *Gracious Cerridwen of Magic and Might*
> *O Goddess of Wonder and Wisdom and Sight*
> *You Who hold Life's keys in the palm of Your hand*
> *And the wisdom of Birth and Death and Birth yet again*
> *I offer this tool to You on this night*
> *Enhance its success; let its magic take flight*
> *Bring it the spark from which all magic flows*
> *Allow it to heal transformational woes*
> *Give it the power to aid meditation*
> *And to soothe and relieve and ease all consternation*
> *And all of the other things that it must do*
> *To serve both of us well as a ritual tool*
> *Your blessings I ask on this cauldron tonight*
> *O Goddess of Wisdom and Wonder and Sight*

The cauldron is now ready for magical use. Wrap it in a soft cloth or pouch and store it away until you're ready to use it.

Magical Theory: Cauldron Exercise
(Week One)

Exercise One: Cauldron Meditation

Hold the cauldron in your lap. (If it's too large or heavy for that, just sit beside it.) Close your eyes and stroke its surface. Think about the cycle of life, and your own life transformation. Think about how many times you are born, die, and are transformed into someone new. Understand that life brings death, and that death is merely a change that brings new life. Then let your mind wander and see what happens.

Perform this exercise every day for one week, and record your progress.

The Besom

The Witch's broom—commonly known as the besom—can be used interchangeably with the wand in Circle. It really shines during the Imbolc Ritual, though, when we sweep away the old (winter) to make room for the new (spring). Some folks prefer to make their own besom using a tree branch and an assortment of special herbs and twigs. However, it's been my experience that, when blessed and consecrated as a ritual tool, a regular broom purchased at the supermarket works just as well. If you really want something special, pay a visit to your local arts and crafts store. They not only offer a variety of scented brooms, but often keep those made of heather in stock. If using herbs that are unsafe for human consumption, be sure to store your broom out of the reach of small children.

When blessing, consecrating, and working with the besom, use the rituals and exercises described in the section titled Wands, then record your progress.

The Black Mirror

The black mirror is an interesting device that's used for scrying and divination. It's traditionally constructed from a piece of concave glass (glass that curves outward like the surface of a sphere). That sort of material can be difficult to come by today, though. For this reason, most black mirrors are either purchased from specialty stores or made from a plain piece of glass held in a picture frame.

If you'd like to make your own black mirror, follow the directions below. The result is an inexpensive tool that's guaranteed to give you hours of divining pleasure!

Materials

1	picture frame with glass in your choice of size
1	can black spray paint
3	tablespoons chamomile, wormwood, or mugwort
1	cup boiling water
	Paintbrush
	Newspaper

Remove the glass from the frame and wash it well with soap and water. Then rinse it under cold running water for three minutes, while willing all negativity and impurity to wash away. Dry it thoroughly.

Place the glass on the newspaper and paint one side using short, even strokes. Allow to dry. Apply two more coats of paint, allowing to dry thoroughly between coats. (No light should be seen through the glass, so apply more paint if additional coats are necessary.) Set aside.

Add the herb to boiling water and let steep for fifteen minutes. (*Note:* Do not drink this tea. Any leftovers should be flushed down the drain immediately!) Strain out the herb and allow to cool. Place the point of the athame in the tea and say:

Pure light from the Universe I now breathe
And into my athame it flows from me
Within this potion it shall remain
Pure light to aid in scrying gain
Positive energies now flow free
As I will so mote it be

Dip the paintbrush into the tea and paint the black side of the mirror. Then, being careful not to scratch the paint, touch your athame point to the center of the mirror and say:

In the name of the Ancients and all good that flows
Only the truth shall this mirror now know

94

It shall guide and protect and be true to me
As I do will, so now mote it be

Using the athame, make an invoking pentagram over the black side. Allow to dry naturally, then return the glass to the frame. Wrap in a soft cloth to keep it dust-free.

When working with the mirror, use Pentacle Exercise Six. Record your progress.

The White-Handled Knife

Although magical theory plays no part in the role of the white-handled knife, it's still a very important tool to the Witch. In fact, it's probably the most frequently used of all Craft tools. From inscribing candles and carving runes to harvesting herbs and plant material, it handles all the mundane tasks that other ritual tools cannot. Fortunately for the Witch, the white-handled knife is not only handy, but easy to acquire. Since the blade is usually single-edged and the only requirement is a white handle, nearly any type of cutlery will do.

Acquire the white-handled knife as instructed for the other ritual tools, taking care not to dicker over the price. As this tool is used for cutting and shaping, it's best to consecrate and bless it during the Waning Moon. Just adapt the blessing and consecration rituals used in the section titled Wands, then keep the knife wrapped in cloth until ready for use.

THE ULTIMATE MAGICAL TOOL

We are, in nearly every sense of the word, our brains. And our brains are what make us magical.

NO MATTER WHAT SORT OF properties we give our ritual implements, nor how powerful they become, they can never take the place of the ultimate magical tool. They can't even function without it. Yet, we tend to question its power. We second guess it, treat it poorly, and sometimes, we even pass it aside as insignificant. It's absolute travesty and we should know better.

This tool isn't something we purchase. It isn't something we cull from a tree or create of our own accord. Yet it holds unsurpassed magical power—magical power so advanced that nothing else comes close. This tool, of course, is the human brain.

Although it has unlimited power and learning ability, we actually use very little of either. It's said, in fact, that we only use one-tenth of its capacity. And with today's technology right at the tip of our fingers, we probably use even less. We barely have to think anymore. We only have to know which buttons to push—and voilá!—we retrieve the technological data that gives us the right answer.

Be that as it may, though, no amount of button-pushing brings successful magical results. Not only must we engage our brains when performing magic, we must use them effectively. We have to be able to think, concentrate, and focus. We must rely on the creative flow. And it's just not as easy for us as it used to be. Sadly enough, we've simply gotten lazy.

Fact is, every member of humankind—regardless of gender, nationality, or race—is 99.9 percent identical. The only thing that sets us apart as individuals is brain-related. It's in our thinking patterns, in the way we process data, and in the way we use that information to its best advantage. We are, in nearly every sense of the word, our brains. And our brains are what make us magical.

This section is, perhaps, the most important one in the entire book. It's designed to exercise your brain, work it to capacity, and whip it back into shape. Yes, it's geared to hone the skills you used to rely on, but seem to have forgotten somewhere along the way. For that reason, please spend some quality time on these exercises. If you do, I guarantee that your success rate will surpass any expectation you might have. If you don't, all your efforts—regardless of how powerful your magical tools or potions—will simply come to naught.

Meditation

In some ways, the brain is much like the body. With the body, for example, we can't build rock-hard triceps or washboard abs overnight. It takes time and practice, routine and regimen. We also have to ease the body into its workout gently. Why? Because plunging right in with rigorous exercise can do serious damage. You could wind up with torn ligaments, or worse. For this reason, professional bodybuilders always take time to perform a series of stretching exercises first. This not only warms the muscles and keeps them supple, but puts the body on notice that it's time to do its stuff.

The same is true of the brain. Especially if it's not used to regular exercise. Its muscles have to be enticed—and sometimes, even cajoled—into maximum performance. Otherwise, confusion sets in. Focus becomes a thing of the past. And you can just forget about willpower, resolution, and determination—they fly right out the window. And so does any hope of magical success.

That's where meditation comes in. It functions as a warmup exercise for the brain, and prepares it for the workout ahead. It stretches lazy muscles, gently bends them to your will, and strengthens them enough to handle whatever comes their way. That, alone, is a great reason to meditate on a daily basis.

There's more: Meditation is one of the most effective stress-relief tools available. Given a chance to do its thing, brain functions come to the forefront. The body relaxes. Muscle tension simply evaporates into thin air. It has no choice. With the brain busy stretching and flexing, it doesn't recognize the need for physical stamina. This gives the body the down time necessary for rejuvenation, and we become healthier people.

While this is all great stuff, the main reason for meditation goes even further. Used on a regular basis, meditation forms a bridge between the conscious world and the spiritual realm. This bridge is important—especially to those who practice the Craft. Why? Because without it, those in the spirit world have no avenue to channel their messages or to help us in any way. And without their assistance, we tend to get into trouble. We experience extreme difficulty when it comes to gaining focus and insight, or finding our way out of the messes we create.

That having been said, please add this wonderful tool to your daily routine. If you're not familiar with the process, please follow the instructions below. They'll put you well on your way to experiencing the most powerful magic you've ever known.

How to Meditate

1. Sit down and get comfortable. (Being comfortable is important here, so if the floor doesn't do it for you, try the couch, recliner, bed, or another piece of furniture that makes you feel cozy.)

2. Close your eyes and relax.

3. Silently say the word "I" over and over to yourself. Focus on the sound of the word and the sound of your breath as you inhale and exhale.

4. Don't worry if other thoughts creep in or get in the way. Just toss them aside and turn your focus back to the word "I" and the natural flow of your breathing.

One final note about meditation. There's no need to worry if you fall asleep during the process. This is very common and simply means that the brain is doing its thing. Spirit messages will still come through, and you'll remember anything that's important.

The Exercises

Remember that the exercises in this section are geared to challenge your brain and work it to its capacity. And because your brain is an entity all its own, it may be more advanced in some areas than others. This means that certain exercises may come easily. Others may prove more difficult. You may even get stuck in an exercise without making the slightest bit of progress. Should this happen to you, don't get discouraged. Just give the exercise the recommended length of time, and mark a star beside it. Then go on to the next exercise. When you've completed it, go back to the one that gave you so much trouble. Master it. You'll be amazed at how easily it comes together for you.

Mental Theory: Thought Absorption
(Weeks One and Two)

Exercise One: Breathing

For this exercise, you'll need to pick a thought on which to concentrate. Some ideas might include improving your study skills, becoming more helpful to those around you, or even breaking a bad habit. Once you have the thought in mind, concentrate on that thought only, then will it to fill the air around you. Breathe the air and absorb the thought with every breath.

Perform this exercise several times daily, beginning with one minute and working up to five. Record your progress.

Exercise Two: Food Consumption

Completely saturate your food with the same thought you used in the previous exercise. Eat slowly while fully focused on that thought.

Perform this exercise with every meal you eat for two weeks. Record your progress.

Exercise Three: Liquid Consumption

Repeat the previous exercise, but use consumable liquids instead of food. Record your progress.

Mental Theory: Focal Retention
(Weeks Three and Four)

Exercise One: Mental Retention

Gather five or six small household objects, then place them on a table in front of you. Close your eyes and visualize only one of the items in perfect detail. Hold the image in your mind's eye for five minutes. If you lose the image, begin again.

   Perform this exercise twice each day, and record your progress.

Exercise Two: Visual Retention

Repeat the previous exercise, but perform it with your back to the table and with your eyes open. The idea here is to be able to visualize the object so fully and completely that it seems to hang in midair before you.

   Perform this exercise several times daily, starting with one minute and working up to five. Record your progress.

(Weeks Five and Six)

Exercise Three: Audio Retention

Hear the sound of a siren in your head. Hear it completely, as if the sound were in the room with you. Hear the sound continuously for five minutes.

   Perform this exercise daily, repeating with the sound of a ticking clock, thunder, knocking, ocean waves, and storm force winds. Record your progress.

(Weeks Seven and Eight)

Exercise Four: Sensory Retention

Focus on feeling each of the following completely: cold, heat, hunger, thirst, gravity, weightlessness, physical energy, and exhaustion. Start with one minute each, and work up to five. If the feeling fades, begin again.

   Perform this exercise daily, and record your progress.

(Weeks Nine and Ten)

Exercise Five: Olfactory Retention

Concentrate on smelling each of the following distinctly: cinnamon, roses, a wet dog, and furniture polish. Start with one minute each and work up to five. If the scent fades, begin again.

Perform this exercise daily, and record your progress.

(Weeks Eleven and Twelve)

Exercise Six: Taste Retention

Concentrate on the taste of each of the following items: sugar, vinegar, salt, and lemon. Focus so completely that you can taste each without even being near it. Start with one minute each and work up to five. If the taste fades, begin again.

Perform this exercise daily, and record your progress.

The Dream Diary

You've been working hard for the last few weeks. You've stretched and flexed and fluxed your mind. Results are beginning to show and your brain is back on track. Now all it needs is a little time—just about a week—to process all the information you've been feeding it. So kick back and relax. Take a well-deserved break. And while you're at it, start a dream diary.

The dream diary is a very important tool, because it brings insight to past and current events in your life. It can also point out personal problem areas, damaging relationship patterns, and all sorts of other issues that can be dealt with easily if apparent at the onset. But that's not all. Kept regularly, the dream diary relieves stress. That makes it a healthy thing to do. And a healthy Witch is a powerful Witch!

There's no right or wrong place to keep a dream diary. Some folks like to use notebook paper and a loose-leaf binder. Others like to use composition books or those of the bound, blank variety. Since I tend to scatter papers on a constant basis, though, I prefer the computer.

The key to successful results is that you have to be able to jot down your dreams just as soon as you open your eyes in the morning. There's no hitting the bathroom first, no grabbing that cup of coffee, and not even a thought of checking your e-mail. It must be the very first thing you do in the morning. Otherwise, portions of your dreams—portions that could be extremely important—tend to get lost in the shuffle. For that reason, I recommend keeping a pencil and pad by your bed. It will always be there, ready and waiting whenever you wake up.

But what if the messages in your dreams aren't apparent? What if they're disguised in symbols, pictures, and disconnected imagery? What then?

Your best bet is to keep a dream dictionary near your diary. There are lots of good ones on the market, and these little jewels make dream deciphering a snap. In the meantime, though, check appendix A in the back of this book. This brief assortment of common dream symbols and their definitions will be enough to get you started. (*Note:* Be sure to write down everything you remember about your dreams *before* defining any symbolism. Otherwise, you may forget to jot down bits of valuable information that complete the dream message.)

Mental Theory: Thought Absorption (Week Fourteen)

Exercise One: Pore Breathing

Lie down on the sofa, bed, or floor, then relax every muscle in your body. Feel all tensions in your body lift, dissipate, and evaporate. Concentrate on one thought (try a healing thought this time, like rectifying an attitude, an emotional issue, or physical health problem) and fill the air around you. Take slow, even, deep breaths, paying close attention to their rhythm and sound. Then visualize the air around you not only entering and leaving your lungs, but through every pore in your body as well.

Perform this exercise daily for one week, starting with five minutes and working up to ten. Record your progress.

Mental Theory: Auto Suggestion (Weeks Fifteen and Sixteen)

Exercise One: Familiar Objects

Sit in a comfortable position and visualize a clock hanging on the wall. Concentrate on the image until you can actually see it. Listen to it tick. Watch as its pendulum swings back and forth. Hold the image for five minutes, then repeat with each of the following: a running stream or brook, an evergreen forest, and a busy street.

Perform this exercise daily, and record your progress.

Exercise Two: Familiar Places

Sit in a comfortable position and close your eyes.

Visualize—in full detail—a place that is both pleasant and familiar to you. Hear any associated sounds, see any related movements, and feel any touches that may be connected. Hold the image for five minutes.

Perform this exercise daily and record your progress.

Exercise Three: Unfamiliar Places

Repeat the previous exercise, but visualize a place you've never seen. Make note of every cloud, every stone, and every tree leaf—visualized in such detail that you will never forget it. Hold the image for five minutes.

Perform this exercise daily and record your progress.

(Weeks Seventeen and Eighteen)

Exercise Four: Animals

Sit in a comfortable position, then close your eyes and visualize a pet, or a farm or zoo animal. Watch how it moves and visualize every muscle twitch. Hear the noises it makes, and feel its touch. When the image is firmly fixed in your mind, wet the animal and smell it. Hold the image for five minutes.

Perform this exercise each day using a different animal and record your progress.

Exercise Five: People

Sit in a comfortable position and close your eyes. Visualize a friend in total detail. Pay attention to clothing, movement, and sound. Pay attention to any conversation you might have. Hold the image for five minutes.

Perform this exercise each day while visualizing a different person. Use friends and family members (both living and deceased), strangers, adults, and children of all races. Watch them work and play, paying attention to anything they might say. Record your progress.

(Weeks Nineteen and Twenty)

Exercise Six: Conscious Visualization

Repeat the last four exercises—Familiar Places, Unfamiliar Places, Animals, and People—with your eyes open. Hold each image for five minutes.

Record your progress.

Mental Theory: Body Control
(Week Twenty-One)

Exercise One: Total Relaxation

Set an alarm clock for five minutes, then lie down on the sofa, bed, or floor. Totally relax your body, but do not go to sleep. Pay close attention to any muscles that twitch, and will them to relax. Work up to thirty minutes of total relaxation.

Record your progress.

(Week Twenty-Two)

Exercise One: Willpower

Practice both personal body and mind control in your daily life this week. If you're hungry, for example, wait an extra ten minutes to eat. Force exhaustion from your mind. Instead of taking a break, keep working at something until it's completed. Remember that you have control over your every movement and thought. Exercise it!

Record your progress.

PART THREE

CIRCLE MAGIC

The Circle goes 'round in our lives and our hearts
As merry we meet and merry we part
Teaching us lessons and doing it right
But giving us stars on the darkest of nights
Granting our wishes and cheering us on
As we follow Its path through the days hard and long
Bringing us friends so that we may play
And laugh and converse as we follow the way
Of the Lord and the Lady and all that it means
As we work toward our goals and reach out for our dreams
At last, It returns us to where we began
But we are now different than we were back then
The magical Circle has changed us—each one—
And we are reborn by the Moon and the Sun
And just when we think the trip's over and done
We find that the Circle has only begun

Dorothy Morrison

THE CIRCLE

The Circle separates the physical world from the spiritual world, and forms a protected area where time and space are completely insignificant.

NOW THAT YOU'VE LEARNED the magical basics, it's time to put it all together. And we do that by casting a Circle. This is important stuff, because nearly everything we do is circle-related in some form or fashion. We get up, go to school or work, and then come home again, completing a circle. We call our relatives the "family circle." People who know our most intimate secrets and love us anyway are referred to as our "circle of friends." Even our basic spiritual philosophies stem from the circle. Take the cycle of birth, death, and rebirth, for example. It's a continuous circle of life without end. The list goes on and on.

That being the case, it's no surprise that all formal Craft rituals revolve around the Circle, too. This Circle is just a bit different from the others we're used to, though. It separates the physical world from the spiritual world, and forms a protected area where time and space are completely insignificant—an area where all of mundanity hangs in suspended animation, and an area where the spiritual world is totally accessible and everything in it is well within our reach. It's a remarkable place to be when you consider the possibilities. And for the practitioner, the possibilities are endless.

Of course, nothing this amazing ever comes about without some doing. We have to plan it, mold it and shape it, give it substance, life, and power. In short, we have to build it. But before we can do that, we have to be ready. And this involves a preparatory cleansing our of bodies, minds, and spirits. Without that, the ritual Circle is useless. Why? Because we are the matrix from which all magic flows. And if we aren't at our best, nothing within the spiritual realm is, either.

For these reasons, please read this entire section before attempting to cast a formal Circle. A quick Circle Setup and Ritual Checklist is provided at the end of the section for your convenience.

Personal Preparations

Preparing for Circle is a personal thing. And if you ask five different practitioners how they prepare, you're likely to get five different scenarios. That's because getting ready for Circle is just as individualized as deciding what clothes to put on in the morning. What works for one person may not be necessary for another, and vice versa. And as you get more familiar with the Circle, you'll develop your own routine, too. In the meantime, though, follow the steps below. They work for everyone, and will give you everything you need for powerful Circle-casting.

- Start by taking a hot bath. Not just a quick one, but a lengthy soak or shower. As you scrub away the physical dirt, visualize emotional and spiritual grime washing away, too.

- Ground and center to clear your head and keep your energy from scattering.

- Spend ten or fifteen minutes in meditation. This is important because it opens and cleanses your spiritual channels and keeps your energy flowing at an even pace.

The Ritual Bath

The ritual bath is not really a bath at all; rather, it's a personal anointing and blessing of sorts that is *always* performed before formal ritual. Preparing the bath, itself, is easy. Just add some herbs or oils that are appropriate to your purpose to a bowl of warm water. Then set it just outside the area where you intend to cast Circle.

Begin by taking a few deep breaths and relaxing your body. Next, stand in front of the bath with your palms facing upward and say:

O Goddess Mother, gentle and mild
Look down and bless me, for I am Your child

Dip your finger in the bath and close your eyes. Anoint your eyelids by drawing a small pentagram on each with your finger. Say:

Please bless my eyes that I might see
Your ways and Your path, and how things should be

Dip your finger into the bath again, anointing your lips in the same fashion. Say:

Please bless my lips so that they may carry
Your words to all people with a voice light and merry

Anoint your breast, saying:

Bless my breast, too—let it be formed in strength
And conviction and courage without bounds or length

Anoint your loins, saying:

My loins, bless as well, for they carry the force
Of all life and creation that flows from Your source

Anoint both knees, saying:

So that I may kneel at Your altar, please bless
My knees; keep them free of all pain and duress

Finally, anoint the tops or ankles of both feet, saying:

And please bless my feet as Your steps they now trace
Keep them on the right path at a straight even pace

Circle Size and Boundaries

Ideally, the Circle measures nine feet in diameter. And you'll hear as many different reasons for this as people you ask. Some will tell you that it's because nine is the numerological digit that relates to wishes. Others will say that it's because the number nine relates to the Goddess. Still others insist that it comes from the mathematical sum of three squared. But even those who agree with the latter don't always agree on the reason. Some are firm in the belief that the sum comes from multiplying the Triple Deities—the Triple Goddess and the Triple God—by each other. The other group says that it's much simpler than that; that it's only a matter of attuning the Circle energies to the formula of karmic retribution, which, of course, is three times three. No one is wrong. They're all good reasons.

The problem with the nine-foot Circle, though, is that most of us don't have that kind of space to dedicate to Circle-casting. Many of us live in small homes or apartments, with little or no outdoor area. And even if we had huge back yards and outdoor space wasn't a problem, we might not really want to inadvertently invite a nosy neighbor into something as private as our personal religious practices.

So what do we do?

It's simple. We just cast a smaller Circle. While nine-foot Circles are roomy—and obviously have plenty of symbology attached—they just aren't necessary to effective magic. The fact is, you can achieve just as much magical success in a two-foot space as you can in a nine-foot space. Size just doesn't matter here. What does matter is that you know where the Circle boundaries are. For this reason, it's a good idea to mark them with something. Candles, flowers, greenery, stones, and shells—or a combination of these items—all work well.

The Quarter Guardians or Watchtowers

The Quarter Guardians or Watchtowers personify the Elements (Air, Fire, Water, and Earth), and each is located in its respective directional area (East, South, West, and North). Each presides over its related area, and together, they not only divide the Circle into four equal sections or quarters, but give the Circle strength. When we stand in the center of the Circle and take our place as Akasha, we provide a perfectly balanced arena from which magic flows.

A symbol of each Guardian or Watchtower—usually a colored candle[1] appropriate to its Element—is placed at the proper direction in the Circle perimeter. Because it's important that Guardian symbols be placed at the exact geographical location that relates to Their Elements, you may wish to use a compass to determine due East, South, West, and North.

The Altar

Because the human factor represents Akasha and is the source from which all magic flows, I like to work in the center of the Circle. Space shortages being what they are, however, it hasn't always been feasible to place my altar there. If this is a problem for you as well, put the altar wherever it is most convenient. Be sure to allow some walking room, though, otherwise you may inadvertently knock over a candle and set the room on fire!

Once you have the altar in place, gather any materials you need for Circle. These include—but depending upon specific ritual requirements may not be limited to—altar cloth and candles, small containers of salt and water, incense and incense burner, cakes and wine, and your ritual tools. Arrange the altar, then light the candles and incense. Hold your hands over the area and bless it, saying something like:

I bless You now that You may aid
The energy flow as magic is made
I cast out negative energy
Leaving only the positive to live and breathe
Within You as we start this rite
Blessed be in joy, and love, and light

Then pick up the wand and draw an invoking pentagram in the air above the altar. Replace the wand and say:

Blessed be, O Creatures of Light
Tools now of magic with power and might

---

1. Alternatively, you may wish to use a stick of incense at the East, a bowl of water at the West, and a container of salt at the North.

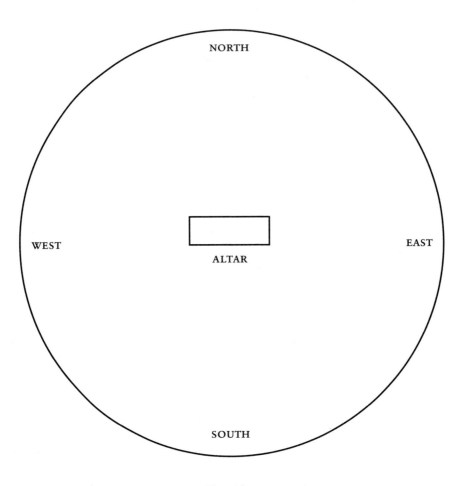

The Altar

Cleansing the Area

Now that the materials are blessed and purified, use them to cleanse the ritual area. Starting at the East with the incense, walk the entire Circle perimeter clockwise while visualizing a yellow vapor rising from the ground. As you walk, say:

By Her fragrant breath—the Air—
By winds blown cold and breezes fair
Be cleansed of negativity
As I will, so mote it be

Leave the incense to burn at the Eastern Quarter, then proceed to the South. Light the candle there and hold it in your hand. Beginning at the South, walk the Circle perimeter again, this time visualizing a red vapor. Say:

By Her burning soul's desire
Of dancing flame and burning Fire
Be cleansed of negativity
As I will, so mote it be

Return the candle to the Southern Quarter, then proceed to the altar and pick up the dish of water. Starting from the Western Quarter, walk the Circle perimeter again while sprinkling the water and visualizing a blue vapor. Say:

By Water that flows through Her veins
The force of storms and gentle rains
Be cleansed of negativity
As I will, so mote it be

Leave the water dish at the Western Quarter, then proceed to the altar and pick up the dish of salt. Starting at the Northern Quarter and sprinkling the salt, walk the Circle again while visualizing a green vapor. Say:

By Earth that is Her body round
By mountain, valley, hill, and mound
Be cleansed of negativity
As I will, so mote it be

Leave the dish at the Northern Quarter. Then, holding your hands palms upward, stand in the center of the Circle area and visualize a purple or white vapor rising from the ground. Say:

I purify this Circle round
By Elements of sky and ground
By Air, Fire, Water, and solid Earth
It's cleansed in love and light and mirth

Casting the Circle

Circle-casting techniques vary from tradition to tradition, from practitioner to practitioner. I've been in Circles that were successfully cast with only one pass around the perimeter. I've also attended rites in which the Circles were "multi-cast," with the passes numbering as many as nine. I like to use three passes in my Circles. Why? Because the number three is very symbolic. It corresponds to the Triple Deities, to karma, and to the cycle of life. Using that number keeps me mindful of each during my rituals, and helps me to be a more responsible practitioner. That being the case, the Circle-casting instructions that follow use three complete casting passes.

Just one last thing before we get started. Since you'll be doing several things at once during Circle-casting—walking, talking, visualizing, concentrating, and so on—it's a good idea to memorize the casting evocation. If you don't, you'll wind up with too many things in your hands and head to be totally effective. And when casting the Circle, effectiveness is what matters most.

To cast the Circle, stand at the Eastern Quarter with the wand. Point the small end away from your body toward the ground. Walk clockwise around the Circle perimeter three full times while visualizing white or neon blue fire streaming from the wand end, burning the Circle boundary into the ground. As you walk, say:

> *I cast you now, O Circle of Power*
> *I conjure your magic to grow and tower*
> *Dividing the world of mundanity from*
> *The world of the ancients and mighty ones*
> *The space where all magic lives and breathes*
> *Where time and place and mundanity cease*
> *Between the worlds, the Circle is cast—*
> *Meeting as one with Present, Future, and Past.*
> *The Old Ones and Young Ones join the night and the day,*
> *And all that's mundane is now swept away.*
> *All Merry Meet, suspended in Time.*
> *The Circle is bound by the words of this rhyme!*

The third pass brings you back to the Eastern Quarter.

Calling the Quarters

Even though we already have the Watchtower symbols in place, we still have to invite the Guardians to join our ritual. Commonly known as "calling the Quarters," this is important for two reasons. First, the Guardians lend the qualities of Their Elements to our Circle and bring it balance. Second, and just as important, once invited, They stand guard over their quarter of the Circle. They watch. They wait. They listen. They prevent any negative energy from entering the Circle; hence the name Watchtower Guardians.

To call the Quarters, begin at the East with your wand in hand. Point the tip of the wand up in the air at due East. Say:

> *Come to us now, O winds of the East!*
> *Whirl and twirl 'til the magic has ceased.*
> *Blow through our hearts, and the energy raise.*
> *Blow away clouds and blow away haze.*
> *the Circle is open—your power please lend.*
> *Your presence is welcomed—we bid you, come in!*

Draw an invoking pentagram in the air with the wand, and visualize the Circle filling with yellow light. Then kiss the wand and proceed to the South.

Call the Southern Guardians in the same fashion by saying:

> *Come to us now, O Southerly fires!*
> *Warm light, pure strength—add flame to desires.*
> *Cleanse and purify all thoughts mundane.*
> *Protect well this Circle with your pure light and flame.*
> *The Circle is open—your power please lend.*
> *Your presence is welcomed—we bid you, come in!*

Draw an invoking pentagram in the air with the wand, and visualize the Circle filling with red light. Then kiss the wand and proceed to the West. Say:

Come now, O waters of the Western port!
Tides rise and fall, and all harm abort.
Wash away troubles and rinse away pain.
Wash over our spirits with your oceans and rain.
The Circle is open—your power please lend.
Your presence is welcomed—we bid you, come in!

Draw an invoking pentagram in the air with the wand, and visualize the Circle filling with blue light. Then kiss the wand and proceed to the North. Say:

Come, Earthly power, to us from the North!
Lend your strength and stability—give your support.
As your soil is fertile, this Circle shall be.
Nourish all works, as you nourish the tree.
The Circle is open—your power please lend.
Your presence is welcomed—we bid you come in!

Draw an invoking pentagram in the air with the wand, and visualize the Circle filling with green light. Then kiss the wand and return to the altar.

Invoking the Lord and Lady

We've already talked about invoking deities—about how They like to be enticed and entertained and about how it's our job to see to it that They get what They want. With that in mind, I've written the following invocations as a starting point. Change them to suit your personal style, or, even better, write your own. The Lord and Lady will definitely appreciate a dose of personal creativity!

Begin by standing in the center of the Circle. Open your arms wide and invoke the Goddess by saying something like:

O Goddess of both Moon and Star
Who rules all planets near and far
Who rules the Earth and all within
Who sets the time our lives begin
Who brings us happiness and mirth
Who gives us value and self-worth

With every loving touch She gives
Unto this plane on which we live
Please descend now from above
And touch this Circle with Your love
And join us in this sacred rite
O Goddess, bring Your love and light

Wait a few moments and see what happens. Sometimes there's a tiny breeze, a flicker of light, or some other physical notice of Her presence. If this doesn't happen, though, don't worry. Deities often make Themselves known in much more subtle ways. There may be no more than a fullness in your heart, a tingle up your spine, or just a feeling of presence.

Then invoke the God in the same fashion, saying something like:

O Lord of Places Wild and Free
Who sows the seed that we might be
Who fertilizes all on Earth
And brings us pleasure, joy, and mirth
Who is the Sun that shines above
Who warms us with His light and love
Who brings good health, prosperity,
And changes all as it should be
Please descend now from above
And touch this Circle with Your love
And join us in this sacred rite
O Lord, please lend Your love and light

Wait a few moments, as with the invocation of the Goddess—about ten heartbeats is sufficient.

The Body of the Ritual

After the invocations of the Lord and Lady, we get to the body of the ritual. It's during this time that we perform the magical work for which the Circle was intended. As there are all kinds of Circles, this work could be anything from emotional or physical healing to ending some sort of planetary crisis, like world hunger. It could involve singing, dancing, or another form of worship. Remember that time is of no consequence within the Circle, so take as much time as you need and perform your work well. Make sure, though, to have all the materials necessary in the Circle area before you cast Circle, otherwise you'll have to cut a gate.

Should you need to exit the Circle, cutting a gate isn't difficult. With your athame, just draw two vertical lines, about two feet apart, in the Circle boundary. Point the tip of the athame at the lower edge of the line on the left, then move the tip until it reaches the top point of the line on the right. Exit the Circle between the lines, taking the athame with you. Move the athame horizontally from right to left between the lines to close the gate after you. Use the same method upon Circle reentry, remembering to close the gate.

Cakes and Wine Blessings and Libation

After performing ritual magic, cakes and wine—or cookies and juice, as the case may be—are blessed and consecrated. To perform this ceremony, hold the plate of cakes out in front of you, and say something like:

> *I conjure You, O meal of grain*
> *Who sprouted in both Sun and Rain*
> *Whose ancient seed fulfills us all*
> *And gains new life where e'er it falls*
> *I bless You in this Circle round*
> *That Your abundance may abound*
> *And feed our world continuously*
> *As I will, so mote it be*

If you are alone in Circle, eat one of the cakes. If others are present, take a bite, then pass the plate to the next person with a kiss and a joyous "Blessed be!" Ask each person to repeat the process until the plate reaches you again.

Place the cakes on the altar, then fill your cup with wine. Hold the cup out in front of you, then say something like:

> *I conjure You, O fruit of vine*
> *Who grew with Wind and Rain and time*
> *From nothing but the light of Sun*

And light of Moon when day was done
I bless You in this Circle round
That Your abundance may abound
And feed our world continuously
As I will, so mote it be

If you are alone in Circle, drink the wine. If not, take a sip and pass the cup to the next person with a kiss and a "Blessed be!" Have each person follow suit until the cup reaches you again. Place the cup on the altar, and set aside two cakes and a bit of wine for outdoor libation. Then share the rest of the cakes and wine with the other participants.

Thanking and Releasing the Deities

After libation, Circle is nearly at close. For this reason, we take some time to thank the Lord and Lady for Their presence. Releasing Them is a sticky situation, though. We don't want to insult Them with a curt dismissal, or even worse, by saying that we're done with Them and it's time to go home. On the other hand, we don't want to detain Them if They have other things to do. A simple solution is to let Them know that we're nearly done with ritual, then leave the decision of staying or going entirely up to Them.

To complete this part of the ritual, stand in the Circle center and hold your arms up in embrace. Then address the Lady, saying something like:

O Goddess of both Moon and Star
Who rules all planets near and far
Who rules the Earth and all within
Who sets the time our lives begin
Who brings us happiness and mirth
Who gives us value and self-worth
With every loving touch She gives
Unto this plane on which we live
We thank You for Your presence here
And hold You in our hearts so dear
And with our love now, You may go
Or stay, if You should deem it so

Then, holding your arms up in the same fashion, address the Lord, saying something like:

O Lord of Places Wild and Free
Who sows the seed that we might be
Who fertilizes all on Earth
And brings us pleasure, joy, and mirth
Who is the Sun that shines above
Who warms us with His light and love
Who brings good health, prosperity,
And changes all as it should be
We thank You for Your presence here
And hold You in our hearts so dear
And with our love now, You may go
Or stay, if You should deem it so

Thanking and Releasing the Quarters

Fortunately, releasing the Quarter Guardians isn't nearly as sticky. Why? As They personify the Elements and lend Their powers to every inner working of our planet, They always have things to do and places to go. Fact is, the Guardians wait with bated breath for us to release Them, otherwise They can't go about Their business or tend to the things that keep our planet operating smoothly. So, don't worry about insulting Them. Just give Them Their leave, and know that They'll love you for it.

To release the Quarters, stand at the East with your wand in hand. Address the Eastern Guardians by saying something like:

O twirling breezes and winds of the East
Who protected this Circle and witnessed all feats
Of magic performed and all blessings poured out
We thank You for coming and gathering about
But now comes the time for this Circle to end
And with love and fond wishes it is that we send
You back to the blustery realm where You reign
Farewell and goodbye 'til we see You again

Draw a banishing pentagram in the air with the wand, then kiss it and proceed to the South. Address the Southern Guardians by saying something like:

O Southern Fires and bright, dancing flames
Who protected this Circle and witnessed all claims
Of magic performed and all blessings poured out
We thank You for coming and gathering about
But now comes the time for this Circle to end
And with love and fond wishes it is that we send
You back to the warmth of the realm where You reign
Farewell and goodbye 'til we see You again

Draw a banishing pentagram in the air with the wand, then kiss it and proceed to the West. Address the Western Guardians by saying something like:

O oceans and rainstorms and streams of the West
Who protected this Circle and witnessed all quests
Of magic performed and all blessings poured out
We thank You for coming and gathering about
But now comes the time for this Circle to end
And with love and fond wishes it is that we send
You back to the watery realm where You reign
Farewell and goodbye 'til we see You again

Draw a banishing pentagram in the air with the wand, then kiss it and proceed to the North. Address the Northern Guardians by saying something like:

O Northern forests and mountains and plains
Who protected this Circle and witnessed all gains
Of magic performed and all blessings poured out
We thank You for coming and gathering about
But now comes the time for this Circle to end
And with love and fond wishes it is that we send
You back to the dark, fertile realm where You reign
Farewell and goodbye 'til we see You again

Draw a banishing pentagram in the air with the wand, then kiss it. Stay at the North and prepare to release the Circle.

Releasing the Circle

Although we cast the Circle in a clockwise motion beginning at the East, we release it from the North by moving counterclockwise. Only one complete pass is necessary to open the Circle. And, as with the casting incantation, you may wish to commit the following to memory. It will definitely make things a lot easier for you during the release rite.

To release the Circle, stand at the North with the wand tip pointed at the ground. Visualize the white or blue flame with which you cast the Circle being sucked back up into the wand. Slowly walk the full Circle perimeter while saying something like:

> *The Circle, though open, remains now unbroken*
> *It remains to protect from all that's unspoken*
> *In Perfect Love and in Perfect Trust*
> *We leave now to do the things that we must*
> *Merry we meet, and now merry we part*
> *Until we meet again with joy in our hearts*

When you reach the North again, stop for a moment. Then go to the center of the Circle area and say:

> *The rite has ended, and I go in love—*
> *With thanks to the Lord and Lady above*
> *With thanks to the Elements and all Others, too—*
> *Merry part and farewell and bright blessings to You*

Libation to the Lord and Lady

Even though you've released the Circle and ended the rite, there's one more thing left to do. It's called "libation to the Lord and Lady," and it's very important. It's a matter of reciprocation, of giving something back to Those Who have given so much to you. Keeping that in mind, gather the cakes and wine you put aside earlier and take them outdoors. Place the cakes on the ground and pour the wine on top as an offering to the Lord and Lady. As you pour the wine, say something like:

By Moon and Sun and Sky above
I offer these in perfect love
By Fire and Earth and Rain and Gust
I offer these in perfect trust
Please take these gifts I offer You
In perfect thanks for all You do
For all the gifts You've given me
O Lord and Lady, blessed be

Circle Setup and Ritual Checklist

• Allow for personal preparation time for Circle.

• Take a ritual bath.

• Gather all necessary ritual materials.

• Mark the Circle boundaries.

• Place each Quarter (Element) candle or symbol at its related direction.

• Bless the altar and any items to be used in ritual.

• Cleanse the Circle area.

• Cast the Circle.

• Call the Quarter Guardians (Watchtowers).

• Invoke the Lord and Lady.

• Proceed with the body of the ritual.

• Bless the cakes and wine, then proceed with Circle libation.

• Thank and release the deities.

• Release the Quarter Guardians.

• Release the Circle.

• Libation to the Lord and Lady (usually outdoors).

• Break down the altar and put everything away.

PART FOUR

WE'RE HAVING
A PARTY

The Wheel of the Year turns around and around
Spinning and rolling with nary a sound
Thirteen new Moons chart a course through the night
Marking each Esbat as they soar in flight
We cherish their fullness, rising so high
Then sing them back down—right out of the sky
The Sabbats, in turn, mark points on the Year
Bringing eight major festivals greeted with cheer
We start out with Samhain, and then we add Yule
Then Imbolc, Ostara, and Beltane do rule
Along comes Midsummer—the peak of the Sun—
And Lammas and Mabon, when harvests are done
And then, once again, the Wheel turns anew
Bringing its magic to all that we do

Dorothy Morrison

THE CELEBRATIONS

Serious ritual and celebration go hand in hand when it comes to the Craft. In fact, we often call our main rituals "festivals."

YOU'VE STUDIED LONG AND learned well. You know how to use your tools, how to flex your brain, how to use the Elements to your best advantage, and how to bend boosters to your will. You even know how to cast Circle. So now it's time for a little fun. A celebration, if you will. It's time for some serious ritual.

Don't groan. Serious ritual and celebration go hand in hand when it comes to the Craft. In fact, we often call our main rituals "festivals." We sing and dance. We eat and drink. We laugh and play and have a good time. There's no room for dull sermons or boring lectures. The Craft just isn't built that way. So, pack up any preconceived notions you may have about ritual and leave them right here. Wiccans not only know how to party—they know how do it up right.

While Craft festivals are many, they mainly boil down to two types: *Esbats* and *Sabbats.* Esbats celebrate the Moon and chart Her month-by-month journey as She moves through the sky. The eight Sabbats, on the other hand, mark the turning of the Wheel of the Year as it rolls from season to season. Complete explanations of these celebrations are in the next two sections.

That having been said, kick off your shoes, grab your ritual tools, and prepare to party. I guarantee you'll have the time of your life!

THE ESBATS

Esbats are important to the Craft, and all Witches celebrate them. It's a little like celebrating a new job, a raise in salary, or some other fabulous stroke of good fortune.

ESBAT IS A PECULIAR word that denotes a minor celebration. Don't be fooled by the word "minor," though. Esbats are important to the Craft, and all Witches celebrate them. It's a little like celebrating a new job, a raise in salary, or some other fabulous stroke of good fortune. It definitely deserves a party, but doesn't require all the frills necessary for a wedding or some other high caliber event—such is the way of the Esbat.

Esbats usually involve the Moon and Her Phases. Some Witches celebrate each Moon Phase—Dark, Waxing, Full, and Waning—as it crosses the sky. Others just celebrate the Full Moon of every month. And for lack of space, that's what we'll do here.

What if you want to celebrate each Phase? What then? Just adapt the following ideas to the proper Phase and write your rituals around the Circle-casting instructions outlined in the section about Sabbats. You'll be amazed at how quickly things fall into place.

The Full Moon Esbat

Full Moon Esbats are important to the Witch. For one thing, the Moon is at Her peak, and that alone is cause for celebration, since Her growth in the sky is a natural phenomenon. But for the Witch, it goes much deeper than that. Because this fullness signifies the pregnancy of Moon coming to term—and there's nothing as powerful as containing a separate life within—Her magical energies are more potent than at any other time of the month. This means that any request—no matter how difficult—has a better chance of being granted during this time. So the Witch not only celebrates the fullness of the Moon, but harvests that energy for magical purposes.

Each Full Moon Esbat centers around formal Circle-casting. And though the Charge of the Goddess is always recited, the Charge of the God is omitted. This is, in no way, a slight against the God. Since the Moon is ruled by the Goddess and it's Her energy that we celebrate at this time, the God simply steps back to let Her shine.

The Moons

Even though there are only twelve months in our calendar year, there are thirteen moons in a lunar year. This means that in every year, two Full Moons fall in one month. The second appearance is commonly known as the *Blue Moon,* and make the month containing it a very powerful one.

Blue Moon occurrences fall sporadically during the calendar year. For convenience purposes, though, I've inserted two Full Moons during the month of January. Please keep this in mind as you celebrate Full Moon Esbats, and understand that the Blue Moon may not appear in January at all, but in a different month entirely.

One other note: Since the Full Moon closest to Winter Solstice is always known as the Oak Moon, I've begun the Esbat Calendar with December. The other Esbats fall in succession.

Explanations and ritual ideas are listed below each Moon. Just add them to your Circle-casting. You'll have a party on your hands before you know it!

December: The Oak Moon

The oak tree has long symbolized the male aspect of Divinity and the natural flow between the worlds of mundanity and spirituality. One reason is that its trunk and branches grow and stretch fervently toward the sky in the physical world, while its roots dig deeply into the hidden planes of the underworld. Another reason has to do with the Holly King, who symbolizes the waning year. The Oak King takes His place at Winter Solstice, and brings the returning light of the newborn Sun with Him. And, of course, there's the mistletoe. Even in the dormancy of winter, this new life sprouts from its branches with berries of white that symbolize the semen of the Lord of the Forest. It keeps us ever mindful that life is always new, always fruitful, and always constant.

As the Oak Moon waxes full in the December sky, remember that you play an integral part in the workings of the Cosmos, just as you do in the world you wake to everyday. Celebrate the return of the Divine Child and New Light by adorning yourself with sprigs of mistletoe, and give candles to others as a reminder that they are each individual flames of the Coming Sun with their own paths to light.

Oak Moon Ideas

- Wear white and yellow to welcome the Sun.

- Decorate altars with holly, mistletoe, and Sun symbols.

- Use white candles and burn Full Moon Incense (see recipe at the end of this section). Alternatively, burn frankincense incense.

- Mark the Circle perimeter with yellow candles or sunflower seeds. If you use seeds, collect them after Circle and put a few aside for spring planting. Scatter the rest outside for the birds.

- Serve gingerbread cookies and apple wine or spiced cider for libation.

- Adorn a candle holder with holly, then secure a white candle inside. Name the candle for any problems or bad habits you've picked up in the last year. Light the candle and release any unpleasantness by saying something like:

I release you now and I am free
You no longer have a hold on me
I banish you with a loving heart
And give myself a brand-new start

Let the candle burn all the way down, then toss the holly on the hearth fire. (If this isn't possible, burn the holly in a fireproof dish and scatter the ashes on the winds.) Know that life has begun anew.

• If this Moon occurs before Winter Solstice, start a perpetual candle to ease the birth of the Sun. Begin by blessing a white or yellow seven-day container candle. Say something like:

Light of the World—Light of the Sun
Bring forth Your warmth when labor's done
Come forth with ease—come without pain
And shine upon the Earth again

Let the candle burn continually, lighting another container candle from its flame before it goes out. Extinguish the last candle on Winter Solstice.

January: Wolf Moon

This Moon is named for the wolf for two reasons: For one thing, it occurs during the time of year when predator food supplies are scarce, and this brings wolves into villages in search of something to eat. The other thing has to do with family and togetherness. Wolves live in packs, and, like humans, they keep the same families for life. They not only depend on their families for love, wisdom, and moral support, they depend on their families for their lives. Without them, many wolves simply pine away and cease to exist.

As the Wolf Moon rises high in the sky, heed the lesson of the predator of the same name. Spend some quality time with both blood-relatives and extended family. Remember that you are who you are because of what they've given. Thank them and show your appreciation. Lend your support. And don't forget that the Gods are family, too. A few words of thanks in Their direction will go far in the coming year.

Wolf Moon Ideas

- Wear shades of burgundy or rose as a symbol of family love and togetherness.

- Decorate the altar with photos of family and friends, mementos of special occasions, and apples.

- Use rose-colored or burgundy candles and burn Full Moon Incense (see recipe at the end of this section). Alternatively, burn pine incense.

- Asperge the Circle with a pine branch to symbolize eternal life and growth.

- Serve sugar cookies and apple juice for libation.

- Spend some time in Circle working on family issues. To mend a rift with a family member or friend, for example, visualize a pink heart. Remove the lower right-hand quarter in your mind's eye. Holding the image, superimpose the heart on a visualization of the person in question. Then chant something like:

> *Remove all doubt—remove this rift*
> *Open this heart that's been adrift*
> *Open now and let me in*
> *And let us never part again*

- This is also a good time to secure an already good family relationship. How? By making a family apple wreath. Start by blessing the apples on your altar (you'll need about six), saying something like:

> *Apples of love, plucked from the tree*
> *Secure our family harmony*
> *Bind it fast and make it true*
> *Do now what I ask of you*

Then slice the apples crosswise to reveal the core and seed pentagrams. Place the slices on a cookie sheet, sprinkle them heavily with cinnamon, and place in the oven at 150 degrees for two hours. While they're baking, cut the hook from a wire coat hanger and fashion a circle from it. When the slices are cool, string them onto the wire and secure the ends by twisting them together. Add a bow if you like. Hang the wreath in a prominent place in your home.

Storm Moon

During the fullness of this moon, we honor the silent winter storms that cover the Earth with frosty ice and snow. Beneath the iridescent blanket, Mother Nature rests and regenerates, renewing Her energy for the growing season ahead.

Since it's important that we renew our energy as well, this is a good time to kick back and relax, and take some time for ourselves. This doesn't just mean physical time, though. We need spiritual time, too. Time to take that inner journey and find out who we are and where we're going. Our growing season will come soon enough. And when it does, we need to be ready.

Storm Moon Ideas

- Wear tranquil shades of blue to honor the Earth's dreaming period.

- Decorate the altar with paper stars and snowflake designs, and symbols of peaceful rest. Try a quilt for the altar cloth.

- Use blue candles and burn Full Moon Incense (see recipe at the end of this section). Alternatively, burn sandalwood incense.

- Leave the traditional wand or athame in storage today, and try casting the Circle with a dream catcher instead.

- Serve butter cookies and hot chocolate for libation.

- Try some dream work of your own. Charge an amethyst and enchant it for prophetic dreaming by chanting something like:

> *Peaceful, dreamy, purple stone*
> *Prophetic dreaming skills, now hone*
> *Bring dream visions now to me*
> *As I will, so mote it be*

Place the stone under your pillow, and prepare for visions untold. Remember to write everything down!

February: The Chaste Moon

Because this Moon waxes full when snow is still on the ground in many places, it holds the power of purity, innocence, and joy. It speaks to the child within us—a reminder of a time when life was simple, a time when a smile went a long way, and everything imaginable seemed possible. Because of this, the Chaste Moon makes us want to laugh, run and play, turn cartwheels, and have fun.

Beneath Her light, we find solutions to messy situations. Barriers flex and give way, and our personal goals are suddenly attainable. The Chaste Moon brings us the opportunity to toss out that which is old and useless. Her coming is the signal to turn a page in life's book and start a new chapter.

Chaste Moon Ideas

- Wear white to honor innocence and joy.

- Decorate altars with white flowers—narcissus and other early bloomers work well.

- Cast the Circle using the wand, cleanse it with burning sage, and use white candles.

- Serve chocolates or chocolate chip cookies and milk for libation.

- Write down requests for inspiration, opportunity, and fresh perspective, then toss them into running water, saying something like:

Take these, Water, as Your guests—
These needs and wishes and requests—
To the Cosmos on Your seas
As I will, so mote it be

- Take steps to simplify your life. If you're a pack rat or have trouble letting go of useless possessions, for example, light a white candle in honor of the Chaste Moon. Then ask for Her help, saying something like:

O Purest Moon of Wondrous Light
Put what's useless in my sight
Help me clear it all away
Simplify my life this day

March: The Seed Moon

With the coming of the Seed Moon, Mother Earth begins to stir. The snow melts, and bulbs—which only yesterday were a tiny sprout of green—burst into full blossom. Squirrels play among the budding treetops, and birds hurriedly search for nest-building materials. Spring has finally come, and with it, a ton of work. All of Nature is busy just trying to keep up.

We, too, feel the need to shake off winter's state of inertia, get up, get out, and do something. Just as it stirs beneath the Earth's surface, the need to create stirs deep within our spirits and wells up inside of us. Her wild and unbridled energy beckons us to till our spiritual gardens and plant them with qualities that better our lives and bring us into harmony with Nature and humankind.

Seed Moon Ideas

- Wear green to honor the Earth's sprouting.

- Decorate altars with wildflowers and spring greenery.

- Use green candles and burn Full Moon Incense (see recipe at the end of this section). Alternatively, burn a soft, floral incense.

- Asperge the Circle with a newly budded tree branch, then set it aside for burning in the Beltane fire later.

- Serve milk and poppyseed rolls or sesame sprinkled bread for libation. Leave a pile of colored threads on top of the outdoor libation spot so the birds can use them for nest-building.

- Bless seeds for spring gardens and flowerbeds. Use a simple blessing such as:

> *Stretch and wake up, little ones*
> *Feel the warmth of Shining Sun*
> *Stir and shake off winter's cold*
> *Sprout and thrive—grow tall and bold*

- Bring seed starter flats into Circle and sow any garden seeds you need to start indoors. The energy of the Seed Moon gives them a wonderful growing advantage.

April: The Hare Moon

As the Hare Moon grows to fullness in the sky, She grants the Earth limitless fertility. Lawns and meadows green with new life. Garden flowers blossom and wildflowers thrive. Even the animals are busy. The need for reproduction rises high, for it's time for their families to grow and thrive.

The fertility of the Hare Moon grows within us, too. We feel the need to be productive, to carry out plans, and to weed out the obstacles that keep us from reaching our goals. Her potent energy calls us to plant and fertilize our spiritual gardens as well as our physical ones. And, of course, love is in the air. With lightened steps and happy heart, we welcome Her coming.

Hare Moon Ideas

- Wear soft greens, yellows, and peaches to symbolize happiness and fertility.

- Decorate the altar with pictures of rabbits, spring greenery and flowers, or anything else that says joy and fertility to you.

- Use green and yellow candles and burn Full Moon Incense (see recipe at the end of this section). Alternatively, burn a fruity-smelling incense like strawberry, peach, or coconut.

- Asperge the Circle with a bunch of wildflowers.

- Weather permitting, hold the Circle outside in the garden area. After Circle, pull any weeds and set out seedlings, plants, and flowers. With each planting, chant:

> *Grow, my friend, so very small*
> *Grow until you're lush and tall*

When planting, don't forget to leave one area of the garden unplanted and unweeded. If left alone, the fairies will tend this section, build homes, and bring magic to your garden. Offer the section to the fairies by saying something like:

> *Fairies, elves, and magic ones*
> *I offer you this spot undone*
> *To live and tend, to laugh and play*
> *Please bless my garden everyday*

- Serve sugared violets (violet flowers first dipped in egg white and then in sugar) or lemon cookies, and strawberry wine or Kool-Aid for libation.

- Bless seeds with qualities you'd like to invite into your life, then plant them. If patience is a problem, for example, you might say something like:

I name you patience—grow in me
As you grow here. So mote it be.

Tend and water the seeds. As they grow, so will the quality within you.

May: The Dyad Moon

The Dyad Moon is an important one because it honors the Lord and Lady's marriage and its consummation upon the Earth. They dance across the land in the joyous splendor that comes from being in love. And the ecstasy and passion of Their mating dance is reflected in every step They take. Flowers burst into full blossom; trees' limbs grow heavy with green leaves; the winds and rains of spring subside now, too, giving way to blue skies and the warmth of the Sun. All is right with the Earth and everyone on it.

On a mundane level, the energy of this Moon provides a good time to finish projects. Productivity levels run high. Goals—even difficult ones—are suddenly within our grasp. And because the Lord and Lady also touch our hearts in Their dancing, love and romance also comes into play. Undoubtedly, this is one of the most powerful Moons of the year for the Witch. It's the time when even the impossible is likely.

Dyad Moon Ideas

- Dress in bright colors and adorn yourself with flowers of the season.

- Use gold and silver candles and decorate the altar with fresh flowers and wedding paraphernalia. Burn Full Moon Incense (see recipe at the end of this section). Alternatively, burn jasmine incense.

- Cast the Circle with a bouquet of flowers tied with colored ribbons. (If you're a solitary Witch, leave the bouquet outdoors on top of the libation area after Circle. If you practice within a group, use it for a wedding bouquet toss instead.)

- Serve cake and champagne or flavored sparkling water for libation.

- Bless fertilizer sticks and garden fertilizer during this Full Moon. Charge them by chanting something like:

> *O Maid and Lord of Moon and Sun*
> *I call you, Ancients. Quickly run*
> *And fertilize these items, please,*
> *So that our plant-life grows with ease.*

- Bless money for fertile growth at this time, too. Charge everyone's change by saying something like:

> *Money multiply and grow*
> *Fertile Maiden, make it so*
> *Let money multiply with ease*
> *With the help of Blessed Be's*

- Ask the Lord and Lady to lend Their passion to other areas of your life, too. It's a good time to enlist Their aid in widening your circle of friends, opportunities, strengthening your capacity for love and compassion, and opening your heart to romance.

June: The Mead or Honey Moon

The appearance of the full, round Mead Moon heralds the end of fertility and the beginning of life anew. Hives fill with honey. Animals give birth and baby birds hatch. Butterflies and cicadas burst forth, too, their shell-like cocoons only a reminder of what they were before. All of Nature is busy now. It's a time of care, nurturement, and transformation.

The Mead Moon brings a time of metamorphosis for us, too. A time to reinvent our lives, change our personal realities, and become what we were meant to be. But before we can do that, we must often change our perceptions of life and see it with a fresh eye. Fortunately, this isn't as difficult as it seems. With the whole world in a state of transformation, it's easy for us to follow suit.

Mead/Honey Moon Ideas

- Dress in shades of yellow and amber to commemorate the honey harvest.

- Use yellow and orange candles and burn Full Moon Incense (see recipe at the end of this section). Alternatively, use frankincense and myrrh incense.

- Decorate the altar with flowers, dandelions, and the transformative gifts of nature. Cicada shells, butterfly cocoons, hatched bird eggs, and shed feathers are all great ideas.

- Serve lemon cookies and honey-sweetened tea for libation.

- Make a Witches' ladder from shed bird feathers to bring personal good fortune for the next twelve months. Just braid together one yard each of red, white, and black ribbon, then attach nine different colored bird feathers by knotting them at equal intervals in the braid. Enchant each feather with a quality as you knot it. For example, while knotting a green feather for prosperity, you might say something like:

Money, money, come to me
As I will, so mote it be

Continue knotting feathers and enchanting them until all are in place. Then tie the braid ends together in a bow and place the ladder between the altar candles saying:

Ring of feathers, braid of three
Bring good fortune unto me

Leave the ladder on the altar until the candles burn completely down, then hang it in an inconspicuous place in your home.

- If you're wondering what to do with your life, set aside some time for meditation. Before beginning, ask for Divine Inspiration by saying something like:

Lady of the Moon, so bright
Look down on me and cast some light
On the path I should follow and what I should be
On the turns I should take to make myself free

Of the life I have now, to gain the life that should be
Mother, I ask you: please help me to see

- Make a personal transformation charm using some of the altar decorations. Just fill a small cloth bag with egg shells, feathers, cocoons, and so on, along with a strand of your hair. Place the bag in front of the altar candles and say something like:

Metamorphical Gifts of Nature, so rare
Quicken my Spirit—lend the courage to dare
To reinvent life into what it should be—
To transform my personal reality—
To refresh my perception and inspire me anew
Do now, O Gifts, what I ask of You

Leave the charm bag on the altar until the candles burn completely down, then carry it with you.

July: The Wort Moon

The Wort Moon is named as such because the Anglo-Saxon word *wort* means herb. That being the case, Her rise in the sky signals the time that herbs have reached their full potential. They stand tall and lush, flowering and fruitful—the product of spring winds and rains and summer Sun. Their aroma fills the air. It lingers and beckons in the summer heat—begging us to choose—begging for inclusion in our magical work.

This Moon also heralds the beginning of our personal spiritual harvests. And because of this, magical efforts seem to come to fruition more easily. Personal psychism abounds, divinatory readings become clear, and dreams are laden with prophesy and vision. For this reason, it's important to give the Spirit World its due, and offer yourself as harvest for its work. In doing this, you'll discover wondrous things about your inner being that you never knew were so. Things that can only make your personal magic more powerful.

Wort Moon Ideas

- Wear shades of orange and green to honor the herb harvest, and adorn your hair with wreaths of herbs or greenery.

- Use orange candles and burn Full Moon Incense (see recipe at the end of this section). Alternatively, burn a mixture of sage, lavender, and rosemary as incense.

- Decorate the altar with bunches of vervain or fresh herbs, tied with ribbons.

- Asperge the Circle with a bouquet of herbs or plants and your favorite herbal tea.

- Serve herbal cookies (just add a tablespoon of lavender or lemon balm to your favorite sugar cookie recipe) and herbal tea for libation.

- Charge herbs and plants in Circle for general magical use. Follow the herbal charging guidelines listed in the section titled Boosting the Magic, but rather than a specific purpose chant, use the following:

> *Plants of wonder—plants of power*
> *Increase in potency by minute and hour*
> *I conjure you now. I charge you with strength*
> *I give you life of infinite length*
> *And boundless magical energy*
> *As I will, plants, charged you be*

- Offer yourself for spiritual harvest by strewing herbs through the yard for the fairies. As you strew, chant something like:

> *All members of the Sprite and Fey*
> *I offer myself to You this day*
> *For spiritual harvest and Your work here below*
> *So that I may flower and blossom and grow*
> *And learn of myself and that up ahead*
> *While working or playing or dreaming in bed*
> *And in return, there is nothing I ask*
> *But that within Your magic my Spirit can bask*

August: The Barley Moon

The Barley Moon also signifies harvest, but Her message is much different than that of the Wort Moon: It heralds the reaping of grain fields. This is important to the Witch because grain holds the mysteries and cycles of life, death, and rebirth within its core. Each kernel is the product of the first grain ever grown. And yet this life renews itself every year to lend its energy and nourish our bodies. There is little else on Earth more ancient or powerful.

In celebrating the Barley Moon, remember that we have much in common with the grain. We are each descended from the first pair of human beings, and their blood still courses through our veins. It sustains and energizes us. It gives us life. Remember, too, that we—each and every one of us—are products of this ancient and fertile life force. And that even though personal ancestry plays a part in our individual identities, we are all related, one to each other, and bound together for all of eternity. Simply put, we each form a link in the chain of eternal life.

Barley Moon Ideas

- Dress in shades of yellow-gold, tan, and warm brown to honor the grain harvest.

- Use yellow-gold candles and burn Full Moon Incense (see recipe at the end of this section). Alternatively, burn patchouli incense.

- Decorate the altar with paper chains, ancestor photos or belongings, sheaves of wheat, and other grains of the season.

- Serve oatmeal cookies or sweet bread, and either alcoholic or nonalcoholic malt beverages for libation.

- Asperge the Circle with a sheaf of grain. After Circle, place it on top of the outdoor libation spot and leave it for the birds.

- Write a thank-you note to one of your ancestors and burn it in incense, letting the smoke carry your message to its recipient.

- Set aside some time to meditate on the chain of life and Universal connection. This is especially important if there are people in your life whom you don't like right now. Then make an effort to mend any relationships gone awry. If you need help taking the first step, say the following prayer to the Mother Goddess.

Gracious Goddess
Who art Maiden, Mother, and Crone,
Celebrated be Your Name.
Help me to live in peace
Upon Your Earth
And grant me safety in Your arms.
Guide me along my chosen path
And show me Your great eternal love
As I strive to be kind to those
Who don't understand Our ways
And lead me safely to Your Cauldron of Rebirth
For it is Your Spirit that lives within me
And protects me
Forever and ever
So mote it be.

September: The Wine or Harvest Moon

This Moon is called the Wine or Harvest Moon because it rises to fullness during the time of the grape harvest. As wine ingestion alters the state of consciousness, ancient people believed that it put them in touch with the Divine Self and its wisdom. For this reason, the Harvest Moon is a celebration of spirit.

As such, the Harvest Moon provides a good time to be quiet, still the body, and let the spirit take over. Pay attention to the wisdom that lives within you. Nurture it. Fertilize it. Cultivate and harvest it. Then follow wherever it takes you.

Wine/Harvest Moon Ideas

- Wear shades of purple and lavender to invoke wisdom, and create the atmosphere necessary to call upon the Divine Self for guidance.

- Decorate altars with flowering herbs and fruit of the season.

- Use purple or lavender candles and burn Full Moon Incense (see recipe at the end of this section). Alternatively, burn sage, allspice, or mugwort as incense.

- Serve graham crackers spread with peanut butter, and grape juice for libation.

- Have a grape-eating contest in honor of Bacchus and Dionysus, Gods of Wine and Harvest. Let the winner bless the participants with a grape juice toast by saying something like:

   With this juice I bless you all
   Big and little, large and small
   By Gods of Wine and Ancient Crone
   May Wisdom be your guide alone

- Weather permitting, go outdoors with a piece of the season's best fruit. Give the fruit back to Mother Earth by burying it in the ground. As you bury the fruit, say something like:

   I offer You this perfect food
   With thanks and love for all You do
   I honor You, O Mother Earth
   Please bless me with Your joy and mirth

- The Harvest Moon also provides a good time for a little brain-teasing spiritual exercise. Think of something and have someone else try to guess your thoughts. Keep it simple and let everyone have a turn.

October: Blood Moon

The Blood Moon gets Her name from the fact that She rises to fullness during the opening months of hunting seasons everywhere. While in ancient times, hunting was necessary to feed families, this is no longer the case. Still, it is a sacred ritual for many people. As hunters, we take full responsibility for the life we harvest. We not only eat the meat, but—just as our ancestors before us—make swift use of the animal's other gifts, giving it an immortality it might not otherwise have.

During this Moon, give thanks to the animals who gave their lives that yours might continue. Include the world of fruits and vegetables as well, for make no mistake: each time one is plucked from the vine to feed you, its life is cut short, too. Then give some thought to how you might immortalize these wonderful, caring creatures in your magic. Apple seeds for love charms, lemon rind for protection magic, and small bones used in efforts of strength and power can really boost results.

Blood Moon Ideas

- Wear shades of red, wine, and scarlet to commemorate the lives lost so that you might live.

- Use red candles and burn Full Moon Incense (see recipe at the end of this section). Alternatively, burn a spicy incense such as cinnamon, nutmeg, or ginger.

- Decorate the altar with animal pictures, autumn leaves, Indian corn, apples, and pumpkins.

- Serve red apple cider (just add a little food coloring) or red wine and ginger snaps for libation.

- Light a red seven-day candle in thanksgiving to the animal and plant worlds, then place it in a window. Invite any departed creatures to visit, saying something like:

> *I light this candle in thanksgiving*
> *For the part you've played in my everyday living*
> *Please come to visit and be my guest*
> *Until this flame subsides in rest*
> *And teach me that which I should know*
> *Until the time comes for you to go*
> *And when it does, I beg you, rest*
> *In peace and quiet 'til your next quest*

- If you have pets, invite them into Circle. Give them a special treat and an extra dose of attention. Let them know how much you love them, and how much their love for you enriches your life. If you don't have pets, make plans to visit your local animal shelter. Play with the animals there, and bring a little joy into their lives.

- Soak some fruit or vegetable seeds in water to soften them, then string them into a necklace. Enchant the necklace in honor of the life cycle and its continuity by saying something like:

> *Seeds with life sealed well within*
> *I honor you for where you've been*

You've been a plant and you've borne fruit
Then back to seed and leaf and root
You've lived and died and lived again
You're life personified without end
And so I thread you on this string
And tie you well into a ring
A circle that is now complete
Like life and death and birth, so sweet
Please aid me in my Circles, round
And in all magic that abounds
I, in return, shall be your friend
And give you back to Earth again

Keep the necklace for one year and wear it whenever you perform magic of any kind. At the end of the year, keep your promise by burying it in the ground and replace the necklace with a new one.

November: The Snow Moon

The rise of the Snow Moon signals the wane of warmth and sunlight, and heralds the coming of the dark months of the year. Mother Earth yawns and stretches. She's tired from all the planting, growing, and harvesting, and prepares to take a long and well-deserved nap. As She settles in, all of Nature follows suit. Even the snow acts in kind. It covers Her with flakes, providing an insulative blanket that keeps Her snug in Her bed, and shields Her from the harsh cold of winter.

We begin to slow down, too. With the Earth at rest, we spend more time indoors. We finish projects and tie up loose ends. We relax and regroup. We contemplate the goodness of the Earth and the fertile abundance She shares with us. We count our blessings. They are many and we are thankful.

Snow Moon Ideas

- Dress in black, purple, navy blue, and other dark colors to honor the sleeping period of the Earth.

- Use purple candles and burn Full Moon Incense (see recipe at the end of this section). Alternatively, burn mugwort or patchouli incense.

- Decorate the altar with onions, garlic, and other vegetables that grow beneath the ground. Use a child's sheet or coverlet as the altar cloth.

- Asperge the Circle with camphor-soaked water. (A bit of Mentholatum dissolved in hot water, then set aside to cool works well in a pinch.)

- Sing a lullaby to the Earth to bring Her peaceful dreams. Try something to the tune of "Brahms' Lullaby," like:

> *Mother Earth, get some rest*
> *Peaceful dreams while You're sleeping*
> *Gain new strength, for the springtime's*
> *Work will shortly come*

- Make a list of all the people who have done something nice for you in the last year. Reflect upon how they've changed your life. Make plans to do something nice for them in reciprocation.

- Make a charm to help tie up loose ends on any projects pending completion. Just place three cloves of garlic and a piece of clear quartz crystal in a cloth bag, and chant something like:

> *Bulbs that grow beneath the ground*
> *Bulbs that grow so white and round*
> *Help me put (name the projects one by one) to bed*
> *Completing their circle in my head*
> *Quartz crystal, do your stuff as well*
> *As I do will, now start this spell*

Place the bag in front of the altar candles and leave it until the candles burn completely down. Then place the bag under your bed to work while you sleep.

Esbat Incense Recipes

If you like the idea of making your own incenses for ritual, try the formulas that follow. Because individual tastes differ, the proportions of each ingredient are left up to you. Just start with a little of each ingredient and experiment until you like the scent, then burn the finished product on a charcoal block.

Full Moon: Anise, lavender, rosemary

Waning or Dark Moon: Anise, camphor, lavender, wormwood

Waxing Moon: Camphor, wormwood

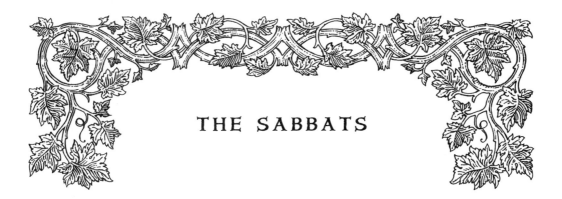

THE SABBATS

*By celebrating the Sabbats we stay in sync with
Nature. We strike a balance between the world of
the spirit and the world of physical. And we do it
all while living our own lives in the present.*

THE EIGHT SABBATS—Samhain, Yule, Imbolc, Ostara, Beltane, Midsummer, Lammas, and Mabon—comprise the major festivals of our calendar year. We celebrate them to honor the change of the seasons and commemorate the Cross-Quarter Days. In doing so, we stay in sync with Nature. We strike a balance between the world of the spirit and the world of physical. And we do it all while living our own lives in the present. It's a pretty tall order, but we're perfectly capable of standing up to the task. After all, celebrating the Sabbats makes for powerful stuff.

It's important to note that all Wiccans aren't necessarily celebrating the same Sabbats at the same time, though. Why? Because unlike the Wheel of the Year in the Northern Hemisphere, that in the Southern Hemisphere turns in a counterclockwise direction. That affects the seasons, which, in turn, affects celebration time. This isn't as confusing as it may sound, though. All it really means is that our neighbors below the equator are always celebrating the Sabbat directly opposite ours; for example, they're having Yule when we're enjoying Midsummer, Beltane when we're celebrating Samhain, and so forth. And together, we make the world of magic go 'round.

That having been said, there's a lot of information in the pages that follow. You'll find a brief history of each celebration, and an explanation of how it applies to our lives. There's a listing of appropriate stones, herbs, and Deities for each festival, as well as individual assortments of ideas you may wish to include in your personal celebrations. The individual rituals, however, are left up to you. There's no need to worry, though. Unless otherwise specified, each ritual requires the same Circle setup and casting techniques described in the section about Esbats. All you have to do is grab some things from the idea lists, and incorporate them into the Circle celebration. Before you know it, you'll have a party on your hands. Guaranteed. *(Editor's Note: Some herbs discussed in this section involve toxic or potentially dangerous materials. Consult a reliable herbal for more information about specific herbs.)*

Samhain
(October 31)

Related Deities: Hecate, Pan, Persephone, Hades, the Morrigan

Related Herbs: Bay leaf, lavender, mugwort, nutmeg, sage

Related Stones: Obsidian, black onyx, bloodstone, amethyst, opal

Samhain [sow'-en] is held on October 31, and is also known throughout the world as Halloween, Hallows, or All Hallows Eve. It's the only festival we observe that deals directly with the dead. For this reason, the Samhain celebration completely defines the role of Death in the cycle of Life, and the importance of its lessons in our personal realities.

In many ancient cultures, Samhain marked the last day of the calendar year. For that reason, it was a time for tying up loose ends and putting things to rest. Grazing days over, herds were gathered from the fields, and either selected for slaughter or put up for the winter. Farmers put their crops to bed, and gave anything that was left back to the Earth Mother by leaving it in the fields to rot. Other tasks were tended to as well: Unpaid debts were rendered in full and arguments were settled. In fact, anything that might mar personal luck in the New Year was not only handled completely, but expediently and efficiently.

Perhaps the main function of this day, however, had to do with those who had died during the year. It was important that they be put to peaceful rest before the coming year, that they were honored and given their due, that their spirits not be allowed any discomfort or displeasure, lest they walk the face of the Earth. And since the veil between the physical and spiritual worlds is very thin on Hallows, it was an excellent day to tend them.

Like our ancestors, we still tend the Dead on Samhain today. We invite them into our Circles, give them peace of mind, and let them speak through us. We honor them, praise their worldly deeds, and give them their due. Then we lead them back through the veil where they may rest until the time comes for them to live on Earth again.

Since the veil is thinnest at Samhain, we also learn much from those in the Spirit World. It's the one time of the year when their messages reach us easily. This is why most people work with divinatory tools at Samhain. While I usually use the tarot for messaging during ritual, others work with runes, pendulums, black mirrors, and so forth. And sometimes, tools aren't necessary at all; the messages are so loud and clear, you'd think that someone was speaking directly into your ear! Be that as it may, many messages come through very quickly, so it's a good idea to keep a pencil and pad near you to take notes. Every message is important, and you won't want to forget anything you've been told.

Samhain Circle Notes

Use an orange or black altar cloth, orange and black candles, and decorate with apples, pomegranates, chrysanthemums, and marigolds. Burn Samhain Incense (a mixture of bay leaves, nutmeg, and sage). Use small jack-o'-lanterns to mark the Quarters, placing Element-appropriate colored candles in each.

Cast this Circle using the athame. After the Circle is cast, go to the Western Quarter and draw an invoking pentagram with the athame to open the gate. Then evoke the Dead by saying:

Spirits walking on this night—
Hearken! Hearken to my call!
Gather in this Circle Light
Enter! Enter! One and all!
Whether you are plant or pet
Or human spirit roaming free
Into this Circle you are let

Blessings we bestow on thee
Please say to us what you must say
And give us all your worries, deep
And we will guide you on the way
To peace and rest and gentle sleep
Spirits walking on this night—
Hearken! Hearken to my call!
Gather in this Circle Light
Enter! Enter! One and all!

Then invoke Pan, the Guardian of the Summerland, and bestow blessings upon the Dead by saying:

O Mighty Pan of the Summerland:
Guardian of the beloved Dead
We pour forth love on those You keep
Safely, in Your peaceful stead
We bless those who have walked the path
That someday, we as well, shall rove
We offer peace unto their souls
While resting in Your arms, below

Perform any divinatory measures that you wish, then return to the Western Quarter with the athame. Say something like:

Blessings be upon you, O wondrous Spirits of the Dead. We thank you for your presence in our Circle and honor you on this sacred night. We beseech you, O Pan, keeper of the sacred Dead, embrace once again those souls within your keep and hold tightly to your breast those that have been lost and wandering. Grant them safe passage to the Summerland, where they may rest peacefully in your strength until they are refreshed and reborn again in perfect love. We bid you each a fond farewell. So mote it be!

Using the athame, draw a banishing pentagram at the Western Quarter to close the Circle gate. (*Note:* Closing the gate is of utmost importance here. Left open,

156

the spirits cannot find their way to the Summerland, and will continue to roam the Earthly plane. They will be left in a state of confusion and could actually wreak havoc in your personal life. It's an aggravation that you and the walking Dead can both do without.)

Samhain Celebration Ideas

- Place a white seven-day candle in the window to guide the Dead to the Spirit World. Light the candle and say:

> *O little flame that burns so bright*
> *Be a beacon on this night*
> *Light the path for all the Dead*
> *That they may see now what's ahead*
> *And lead them to the Summerland*
> *And shine until Pan takes their hands*
> *And with Your light, please bring them peace*
> *That they may rest and sleep with ease*

- Because this is a time of endings, magic is often performed to get rid of unsavory personal characteristics or break bad habits. Just write the character trait or habit on a piece of paper, light it, and toss it into the cauldron or a fireproof dish, saying something like:

> *I burn this trait now from my life*
> *Upon this sacred Samhain night*
> *It is gone from me at last*
> *Just a memory from the past*

- Since this is the beginning of the dark time of the year, say goodbye to the Sun and wish Him well as He rests now until the time of His rebirth on Yule. At the end of ritual, include a farewell by saying something like:

> *Farewell, Dear Sun, Who warms the Earth*
> *Who, with Your Light, brings joy and mirth*
> *Close Your eyes now—go to sleep*
> *Rest peacefully in Darkness, deep*

Until the Yuletide fest begins
And You are born to us again

Then extinguish all candles to signify His absence.

• To feed the Dead on their journey and gain their blessings, either leave or bury a few apples and a pomegranate outdoors after libation. As you leave the fruit, say something like:

O Fruit of Death and Fruit of Life
Fruit that eases mortal strife
Ease the hunger of the Dead
Until They reach Their final stead
Be food enough for everyone
Until Their journey's fully done

Yule
(December 21 or 22)

Related Deities: Mother Berta, Father Winter, Santa Claus, Kriss Kringle, St. Nick, the Kings of Holly and Oak

Related Herbs: Chamomile, rosemary, ginger, sage, cinnamon

Related Stones: Quartz crystal, blue sunstone, emerald, ruby, sapphire

A solar festival, Yule falls on the first day of winter—the day that the Sun is reborn to warm the Earth again.[1] And even though some of the traditions are a lot like the Christian Christmas, its origins are much more ancient. In fact, the ancient Egyptians started this festival over four thousand years ago with a twelve-day party to celebrate the rebirth of Horus—the son of Isis and Osiris—whose Earthly guise took the form of the Sun. Because they saw greenery as a magical growth tool—and they wanted the Sun to grow and stay in the sky longer—they

---

1. Since Yule is the celebration of the Winter Solstice—the first day of winter—festival dates vary year to year.

used it to decorate everything in sight. Soon, the Egyptians prospered and news of their Sun-welcoming festival spread through Mesopotamia.

That being the case, it wasn't long before other countries followed suit. Incorporating occasional gifts, the Babylonians began to worship the newborn Sun with a celebration called Zagmuk. The Persians and Greeks started their own solar celebrations, too—both were called Sacaea. But in wasn't until the ancient Romans got in on the act that things really started popping. They named their festival Saturnalia, and included candles, singing, gourmet feasting, and lavish gift-giving. And with that, Winter Solstice celebrations spread throughout Europe and the Yule festival, as we know it today, was born.

Yule comes from the Scandinavian word *Jul*, meaning wheel. And though there are many solar themes associated with this festival, the most common in our celebration is the battle between the aging Holly King, who represents the darkness of the old year, and the young Oak King, who symbolizes the light of the new year. Sometimes the battle is reenacted during ritual. In this case, the old king is symbolically slain, and the Oak King takes his place on the throne to rule. More often than not, though, the tale is simply told during the lighting of the Yule log. And with its lighting, we encourage the Sun's easy birth, welcome it back to the Earth, and ask it to cast its warming, healing rays upon us once more.

Yule Circle Notes

Use a white altar cloth, and decorate with evergreens, poinsettias, rosemary, holly, mistletoe, and ivy. Use red, white, and green candles to symbolize the bloodshed of birth, the innocence of new life, and the growth process, respectively. Burn Yule Incense (a mixture of chamomile, ginger, pine, and sage). Mark the Circle perimeter with evergreen boughs, and use tiny, living, decorated trees at the Quarters. (Decorations should relate to the appropriate Element.)

Cast the Circle using the athame. Release it using the wand.

Yule Celebration Ideas

- Start your celebration well before dawn, so you can be a part of the Sun's birthing process. Kick off the ritual with an apple juice toast to the Holly King, saying something like:

Winter day of longest night
Step aside now for the light
Thank you for the things you've brought
That only darkness could have wrought

Then name all the gifts of darkness you can think of—regeneration, peace, dreams, organization, quietude, and so on—before drinking the juice.

- To ensure good luck and prosperity in the coming year, anoint a bayberry candle with vegetable oil and roll it in dried chamomile. Light the candle and allow it to burn down completely.

- Make a Yule log from a piece of oak and decorate it with evergreens. Light it, saying something like:

Old King, we thank You for all You've done
For lessons learned, and victories won
We must, however, bid You adieu
For Your reign is finished—'tis over and through
Come forth, Young King of newest light
Be born with ease; grow strong and bright
Gain strength and stature in the sky
Shed Your warmth on us now from on high

Be sure to save an unburned piece to start next year's log. Save some of the ashes, too. They make terrific boosters for every type of magic.

End the ritual with an orange juice toast to the Sun, saying something like:

O Newborn Sun of love and light
Rise quickly now, rise high and bright
Gain power in the sky above
We grant you our support and love

- After ritual, collect all the evergreen decorations you used there and put them away. You'll need them at Imbolc.

Imbolc
(February 2)

Related Deities: Brigid, Brid, the Maiden, the Spring Goddess, the Young Lord

Related Herbs: Angelica, basil, bay leaves, myrrh

Related Stones: Quartz crystal, opal, moonstone, aventurine, sunstone

Although we call this celebration Imbolc [im'-bolk] or Candlemas, you probably know it as Groundhog Day. The word *Imbolc* literally means "in the belly." No other name could be more appropriate, for this festival is a celebration of the first fetal stirrings of the Earth as She responds to the wake-up call of spring. And although this is definitely a fire festival, the emphasis here is not so much on warmth as it is light. Why? Because the light is necessary to guide spring's path so it doesn't get lost, or even worse, forget to renew the Earth with its greening. This is also the reason why all candles to be used in magical efforts for the next twelve months are blessed at this time.

One theme for this festival surrounds the preparation of Brid's or Brigid's [breeds] Bed. This is usually a basket filled with raffia or Easter grass that's decorated with ivy and white satin ribbons. Then a corn dolly dressed as a bride is placed inside along with a symbol of masculinity. This represents the first intimate encounter between the Maiden Goddess and the Young Lord, and ensures fertility in the months ahead.

The most common theme, however, is that of purification. It's symbolized by the sweeping of the Circle, and is a little like spring-cleaning for the body, mind, and spirit. We get rid of what's no longer of use to us—bad habits, old ideas, preconceived notions, unsavory character traits, and so forth—to make way for the new and exciting things to come. We open our minds and spirits to change and all it entails. And in doing so, we embrace new life—a fertile, wonderful life where doors open and things fall into place, a life that greens our hearts as well as our spirits, the life that we truly want to live.

Imbolc Circle Notes

Use a brown altar cloth to symbolize the Earth, and decorate with narcissus, daffodils, crocuses, hyacinths, or other seasonal flowering bulbs. Anoint white candles with musk oil and place them in ivy-covered candle rings. Burn Imbolc Incense (a mixture of angelica, basil, bay leaves, and myrrh).

After casting the Circle with the wand, use the besom to sweep the perimeter. As you sweep, say something like:

> *With this besom filled with power*
> *Sweep away the old and sour*
> *Sweep away the chill of death*
> *As winter draws its last cold breath*
> *Round, round, round about*
> *Sweep the old and useless out!*

After libation, bless the candles for the coming months by saying something like:

> *I bless thee creatures of wax and light*
> *And cast out negativity*
> *Serve your purpose, flaming bright*
> *Infused with magic, you shall be*
> *Instruments of light and strength*
> *Wick and wax though you may be*
> *I give you life of needed length*
> *To aid in creativity!*

Continue Circle in the normal manner.

Imbolc Celebration Ideas

- Turn on all the lights in the house for a few moments to guide the path of spring. If you like, burn a votive candle in each room instead.

- Tie three small ears of corn together with a white satin ribbon, then wrap the bundle in a white doily to represent Brid. Use a clear quartz crystal point to represent the Young Lord. As you place them in the basket, say something like:

> *The Maid and Lord now bring us light*
> *The winter dies, and all is bright!*
> *And as They lie in bed so near*
> *The frozen ground does disappear—*
> *For Their love brings fertility*
> *To the Earth again; so mote it be*

- Burn all evergreen decorations from the Yule ritual. This ensures good luck in the coming year.

- Tie small bundles of straw together with pieces of black ribbon. Name each bundle for something you want to remove from your life, then burn it in the cauldron.

- After libation, walk outdoors for a few moments. Remember the warmth of spring. Then trace the male and female symbols (the symbols for Mars and Venus) on the ground and enclose them in a circle. Say something like:

> *Encased in Sun, Your light shall shine*
> *And guide the spring toward greening time*
> *And as your hearts both melt in love*
> *The light grows stronger from above*

Ostara
(March 20 or 21)

Related Deities: Eostre, the adolescent Spring Maiden, the adolescent Spring Lord

Related Herbs: Jasmine, rose, violet

Related Stones: Moss agate, green moonstone, orange calcite, rose quartz

Also known as Vernal or Spring Equinox, Ostara [o-star'-a] marks the rekindling of life within the Earth and the renewal of fertility to our spiritual lives. This fertility festival and the Christian Easter celebration both get their names from the free-spirited goddess, Eostre. Legend has it that while entertaining a group of children, she once turned a bird into a rabbit. To the amusement of the children, the bewitched animal laid colored eggs. Her story is the basis for the Easter Bunny, spring egg hunts, and most other traditions associated with this holiday.[2]

Eostre's story aside, the egg is an excellent symbol for the spring celebration. The egg white represents the all-encompassing nature of the Goddess while the

---

2. Since Ostara is the celebration of the Spring Equinox—the first day of spring—festival dates vary year to year.

golden yolk represents the virile qualities of the Sun God. The symmetrical outer shell binds the two together, sealing Their fertility and Their perfect love for one another.

From a more mundane angle, all animal life comes from eggs. Fish, fowl, amphibians, and insects lay them. Mammals conceive when sperm cells penetrate them. If you wanted to stretch the imagination somewhat, you could say that vegetation sprouts from eggs, too. Being embryonic and shell-covered, seeds are egg-like in nature. For these reasons, eggs provide a prime fertility symbol for the Ostara ritual. For use ideas, try some of the tips in the Ostara Celebration Ideas.

Ostara Circle Notes

Use a green altar cloth, pastel colored candles, and decorate with wild flowers or flowers of the season. Burn Ostara Incense (a mixture of orris root, jasmine, rose, and violet petals). Use small baskets of appropriately colored eggs to mark the Quarters.

Cast the Circle with the wand. Alternatively, use a flowering branch of some sort. Dogwood, cherry, and pussy willow branches all work well.

Ostara Celebration Ideas

- Serve deviled eggs and milk for libation instead of cakes and wine.

- Using a white crayon, label boiled eggs with qualities you'd like to add to your personality or life. For example, you might label one with prosperity, another with kindness, and so on. Dye each egg an appropriate color, bless it during the ritual, and eat it. Know that the quality's spiritual seeds have been planted within you and will flourish throughout the year.

- Plant an uncooked egg at each corner of your property to ensure a fruitful home life. As you put each egg in place, say something like:

Fertile egg of ancient life
Bring joy and laughter—ease all strife—
And with your great fertility
Grant perfect love and harmony
To all who live within these bounds
Be they person, thing, wild life, or hound

- Thoroughly beat three eggs and blend them into a quart of milk. Bless the mixture by saying something like:

> *Fertile measures of the Earth*
> *Meld and mix with joy and mirth*
> *Bring all you touch fertility*
> *As I will, so mote it be*

Then use it to asperge and bless any yet unplanted garden areas. (If you don't have an outdoor space but intend to grow seeds indoors, put the mixture in a spray bottle and thoroughly mist the inside area of the pots.)

As you sprinkle the area, say something like:

> *Milk and egg, now fertilize*
> *This plot of Earth beneath the skies*
> *I bless this place by the Lord and Maid*
> *Soil grow rich in sun and shade*

- Weather permitting, hold the rite outdoors in the garden space. After the ritual, mark out the planting area and till it thoroughly, working the soil until it's smooth and supple. Then spread out a blanket and have a picnic on the spot. Make plans for planting the garden.

Beltane
(April 30 and May 1)

Related Deities: May Queen, Stag Lord, Jack-in-the-Green, the Green Man

Related Herbs: Frankincense, roses, lemon balm, lemon thyme

Related Stones: Quartz crystal, sunstone, orange calcite, malachite

Beltane is a fire and fertility festival in which we welcome summer and coax it to join us. Since this festival was first celebrated by the Celts—and they figured days from sundown to sundown—this celebration begins at sunset on April 30 and continues through sunset on May 1. The word Beltane comes from the Welsh words *tan* (meaning fire) and *Bel* (the name of the Welsh Sky God). Combined, the words mean "fire in the sky," creating a wonderfully appropriate name for invoking the spirit of summer.

Traditionally, two babies—one of each sex—were selected annually to be trained for the roles of the Stag Lord and the May Queen. Their time came at the age of fourteen, and the boy, in his role of the Stag Lord, ran with the deer. At some point, the dominant buck, or Great Stag, of the herd would sense the intruder, and it was up to the Stag Lord to overcome him. Returning victorious and undamaged, the Stag Lord then mated with the May Queen in symbolic consummation of the marriage between the God and Goddess, bringing fertility to all of the lands around them.

Although this ritual was of major importance to the celebration of Beltane, it by no means was the only custom with which the festival was associated. The celebrants danced around the Maypole in a clockwise motion—the direction of the Sun's journey across the face of the Earth—while weaving the flowers and vines tightly to its surface. The pole maintained its reign in the center of the village until it was replaced the following year, at which time it was split into logs to fuel the new Beltane fire.

The Beltane fires burned throughout the entire celebration as a symbol of the Sun's lengthening reign in the sky. Livestock was driven between two bonfires during the festival, as a measure to protect them from disease in the coming year. The frail and sick also passed between the fires to obtain the Sun's healing blessings. This procedure was very important, for sick people are seldom fruitful, and to ancient people, fertility was a matter of life and death. Abundance of the land and livestock ensured a plentiful food supply, and fertility of the people meant that the procreation of humankind would continue without fail.

Although an ancient festival, Beltane is still celebrated today the world over, by Pagans and Christians alike. The Dance of the Maypole is still a common practice as the spirit of summer is "conjured" in, and people everywhere adorn themselves with floral delights and brightly colored clothes. There are games for the children, and it is a common practice for couples to jump over the bonfire for fertility and general good luck. Gardens are blessed and May baskets are delivered to the elderly with cheer and good tidings. It is still a day of frivolity, sensuality, and delight—but it is also a good day to reflect upon our ancestors and give thanks to the Lord and Lady for our good fortune.

Beltane Circle Notes

Celebrate this ritual outdoors near a living tree. (If that's not possible, bring a small, potted tree or plant indoors.) Use a dark green altar cloth and decorate with flowers of the season. Anoint green candles with floral-scented oil and place them in flower-covered candle rings. Burn Beltane Incense (a mixture of crushed almonds, frankincense, and rose petals). Mark the Circle perimeter with flower petals.

Cast the Circle using the wand. Alternatively, use a bouquet of flowers tied with colored ribbons.

Beltane Celebration Ideas

- Light a fire in the fireplace at sundown to invoke the Sun God. Keep it going until sundown on May 1. If you don't have a fireplace—or it's too hot for a fire—light a large white or yellow seven-day candle. When lighting the fire or the wick, chant:

> *God of Sun, Fire in the sky*
> *Light the Earth and warm the night*
> *Warm our spirits, hearts, and hands*
> *Shed Your light upon this land*

- Using a coat hanger wire as a base, make a door wreath of fresh greenery and flowers. (Just shape the wire into a circle, then attach small bunches of flowers and greenery with floral wire. Finish off with a pretty bow.) Decorate the house with any leftover plant materials.

- If you have a yard and can dance the Maypole outside, obtain a closet pole from your nearest hardware store or lumber yard. These make excellent Maypoles and are very inexpensive. Cut ribbon streamers twice the length of the pole and fasten them securely to the pole top with small nails or brads. Pound the pole into the ground in the center of the yard.

- Hold a food drive and make food baskets. Bless them by chanting:

> *Fire of Sky and Fire of Sun*
> *End all hunger—be it done*

Take the baskets to those less fortunate than you. Deliver them to homeless shelters or to people living on the streets. You can also contact local church personnel for lists of families needing food.

- Serve an evening meal of breakfast foods to invoke the fertility of the Sun God. Pancakes, eggs, milk, cheese, bacon, sausage, and honey are good options. Fix an extra plate for the Sun God, and leave it outside in the East when supper is finished.

- Before going to bed, say the following prayer for Universal fertility:

Lord and Lady, Growing Sun
Bless us in our work and fun
Bless the land and animals, too
Bless the crops and morning dew
Bless all that live upon this land
Bestow Your great abundance and
Fertilize all that we do
This we humbly ask of You

Midsummer
(June 21 or 22)

Related Deities: Mother Earth, Father Sun, the fey and fairy-folk

Related Herbs: Rue, roses, vervain, trefoil, St. John's Wort, chamomile, lavender, mugwort

Related Stones: Amethyst, malachite, golden topaz, opal, quartz crystal, azurite-malachite, lapis lazuli

Also known as Summer Solstice, Litha, or St. John's Day, this festival is the celebration of the first day of summer, the longest day of the year. Since the Sun reaches its peak strength on this day, the God takes His place as Father Sun. The Goddess, in turn, becomes Mother Earth. And it's in these guises that both work long and hard to keep the Earth green, lush, and bountiful.[3]

---

3. Since Midsummer is the celebration of Summer Solstice—the first day of summer—festival dates vary year to year.

For this reason, Midsummer isn't just a solar festival—it's a celebration of service, of sharing, and of giving our due to the planet. It's a celebration of doing our parts to prepare for the harvest season, and it's not just the agricultural harvest that concerns us at this time. *We* will be harvested, too, and we must be ready. This involves sharing with our communities, giving back to those who have helped us, and performing random acts of kindness toward those less fortunate than we are.

Fortunately, we have help at Midsummer. With the Sun at His peak, so are the fairies and fey. And we are the objects of their labor. Sometimes disguised as lightning bugs, They flit to and fro, greening our hearts and tending our spiritual gardens. They lighten our steps and fill us with the warmth of joy and laughter. With the fey working overtime to point us in the right direction, we see things in a different light. And suddenly, it's not as difficult to do nice things for other people; in fact, it's downright easy.

However, everything has its price, and so does the help of the fey. Just as we honor the Lord and Lady on Midsummer Day, we must pay homage to the fairy-folk on Midsummer Night. To do otherwise is just asking for trouble and undue chaos. Think I'm kidding? It's all chronicled in one of the most famous literary works of all time: *A Midsummer Night's Dream,* by William Shakespeare.

Midsummer Circle Notes

Use a green or white altar cloth, and burn blue and yellow candles. Decorate with fresh herbs, flowers, and seasonal greenery, and wear some in your hair. Burn Midsummer Incense (a mixture of chamomile, lavender, mugwort, and rose petals).

Tie tiny bells to the wand with colored ribbons to appease the fey, and use it to cast Circle.

Midsummer Circle Ideas

- Rise before dawn and welcome the Sun King at daybreak. As the Sun appears on the horizon, toast him with orange juice, saying something like:

Mighty Sun King, round and bright
I welcome You into my life
I honor You upon this day
As You warm us all with golden ray

- Decorate trees with solar symbols tied by yellow and blue ribbons. As you tie each symbol, say something like:

> *Mother Earth and Father Sun*
> *We honor You for a job well done*
> *The Earth has greened and so have we*
> *You've brought back perfect harmony*
> *Mother Earth and Father Sun*
> *Pour out Your blessings one by one*
> *Upon the Earth and on us, too*
> *As we tie these ribbons of yellow and blue*

- Kindle an outdoor bonfire of oak, fir, and St. John's wort, and jump over it to bring good health and good luck for the rest of the year. (Alternatively, kindle the fire in your cauldron.) As you jump the fire, say something like:

> *Good health and fortune await me*
> *As I will, so mote it be*

- Make beeswax herb candles in Circle. Just take a sheet of beeswax and sprinkle a tablespoon of herbs on top. Place a wick on the outer edge and roll up tightly, while chanting something like:

> *Herb and wax, now meld and mix*
> *Within you, magic I now fix*

Then offer them for the work of the Lord and Lady, and the fey, by saying something like:

> *These candles are my offering*
> *To ease the workload as You bring*
> *The seasons into play each year*
> *I offer them with love and cheer*

Burn one candle with the change of every season.

- Leave a plate of food outside for the fairies. Drizzle it with honey, and say something like:

Fey and Fairy-folk alike,
Leprechauns and Flitting Sprite
I pay due homage now to Thee
Upon You, may all blessings be

Lammas
(July 31 and August 1)

Related Deities: Ceres, Demeter, the Corn Mother, Lugh, John Barleycorn, the Green Man

Related Herbs: All herbs and all grains (corn, wheat, milo, rice, oats, and so on) are sacred.

Related Stones: Tiger-eye, golden topaz, opal, citrine, ametrine

Lammas—or Lughnasadh [loog'-na-sod] as it's sometimes called—marks the middle of summer and the beginning of the harvest season. We pay homage to the Sun God, Lugh, for His role in the Earth's fruitfulness. We say goodbye as He wanes in the sky. This is not a time for sadness, however, for His seed lives on in the Mother's womb. And the Mother is at Her abundant best. The fruit of Her labor is everywhere, and we gather to reap Her bounty.

Because of its connection with the grain deities, many folks think that Lammas is just a grain harvest festival. But nothing could be further from the truth. Vegetables, ripe and plump on the vine, beg to be picked. Onions and garlic await unearthing. Herbs—especially those specifically chosen for magical use—are at their most potent now. We've come of age, too, and the time of personal harvest is upon us.

That being the case, it's not only important to reap the fruits of the Earth now, but as the Mother's children, to offer ourselves for harvest as well. By doing so, we will be chosen to carry on Her work in many forms and fashions. We know that this work won't always be easy. But we also know that the Mother will bless us many times over for the parts that we play, and that these blessings will always outweigh any effort that we put forth.

Lammas Circle Notes

Use a yellow or yellow-orange altar cloth, and green, yellow, or orange candles. Decorate with bunches of herbs, sheaves of grain, ears of corn, and small baskets of fruit and vegetables. Burn Lammas Incense (a mixture of frankincense and sunflower petals or heliotrope).

Cast Circle using the athame.

Lammas Circle Ideas

- Kindle a Lammas fire of herbs and wood to commemorate the Sun's passing. Say goodbye to the Sun by saying something like:

> *We thank You God of Sun and Light*
> *For warming us from dawn 'til night*
> *For fertilizing all on Earth*
> *For bringing us Your cheer and mirth*
> *For laughter, joy, and shining ray*
> *For guiding us along our way*
> *And as You go, we hold You dear*
> *Until the winter brings You near*
> *And with the Yule You're born anew*
> *Goodbye, dear Sun, we shall miss You*

- Thank the Mother for Her bountiful gifts by blessing the onions, garlic, and grain staples in your kitchen (flour, cornmeal, oatmeal, and so on). Line them up on the altar or counter, place your hands over them, and say something like:

> *We thank You, Mother, for these gifts*
> *For meal and bulbs and that which sifts*
> *Please bless these items with Your grace*
> *And hold them dear within their space*
> *So as we eat, Your blessings flow*
> *Within, without—from head to toe*

- Bake magical bread in celebration of the harvest. This doesn't have to be difficult or take all day. Just use frozen bread dough, and knead in a tablespoon or two of fresh herbs when it thaws. (Basil, oregano, dill, parsley, and chives are all good choices.) As you eat the bread, say something like:

Cycle of Life contained herein
Birth and death and birth again
Help me to understand my role
In life, and help me cleanse my soul
So I may walk this path with ease
As I will, so mote it be

- Make the corn dolly for next year's Imbolc. Just acquire three ears of corn and tie them together as directed in the Imbolc Celebration Ideas. Bless the dolly by saying:

Seeds of life that burn and thrive
Seeds of plenty come alive
By Sun and Earth this spell fulfill
Become now Bride, who melts the chill

Put the dolly in a safe place to await the Imbolc celebration.

- Perform prosperity magic for the coming months by making a Witches' bottle. Just gather together a small bottle with a tight-fitting cork, a fish hook, some clover, a bit of cinnamon, and a few coins. As you place the materials in the bottle, visualize money coming to you from all directions. Cork the bottle and seal it with a bit of wax from the altar candles, then enchant it by saying something like:

Money come alive and grow
Pour down on me both high and low
By herb and hook and glass and coin
Prosperity and I now join
Paper money and coins that shine
Come to me, for you are mine

Bury the bottle near your front door. If that's not possible, set the bottle in a place where it won't be disturbed.

Mabon
(September 20 or 21)

Related Deities: Mabon, Modron, Persephone, Demeter

Related Herbs: Marigold, sunflowers, hibiscus, rose petals, myrrh

Related Stones: Amber, clear quartz, tiger-eye, citrine

This festival is named for the Welsh God, Mabon [ma'-bon], Whose name means "Great Sun." The story goes that He was kidnapped from the Great Mother (Modron) when He was but three days old, and taken to the Underworld to prevent His light from shining on the land. He was much smarter than the Lord of the Underworld thought, though. During His stay within the Earth, He not only gathered His wits, but the personal strength and momentum necessary to become new seed. He knew His rescue was at hand, and when the time came, He'd need all the power he could muster to fertilize the barren Earth and green it once more. Looking at it from this angle, Mabon is, in many ways, the male counterpart of the Roman Goddess, Persephone, Who—snatched from the Earth by Hades (the Lord of the Underworld)—shares credit for the coming of the dark time of the year.

Celebrated at Fall Equinox,[4] Mabon marks the first day of autumn and the second harvest periods—both agricultural and personal. As with Lammas, it's a time to celebrate the Earth's bounty and thank Her for the blessings She brings us. For this reason, it is often called the "Witches' Thanksgiving." We tend to set lavish tables, plan huge meals, and gratefully partake of every delectable morsel available.

But there's more to it than that. Because of Mabon's association with the Underworld, it's also a great time to remember our ancestors, and those who have gone before us. To thank them for the blood that courses through our veins, for the traits that we share from their personal gene pools, and for the gifts they have given us that make us the fabulous specimens of individuality that we are.

Because of this, Mabon is a time of total thanksgiving—a time when we give thanks for all that we have, for all that we are, and for all that the future holds,

---

4. Since Mabon is the celebration of Fall Equinox—the first day of autumn—festival dates vary year to year.

not only for us personally, but for those yet unborn. It is a time to reflect on the joys of community, personal freedom, and the wonders of the human species as a whole, and a time to count our many blessings, and give thanks to everyone who's made them happen.

Mabon Circle Notes

Use a deep orange or burgundy altar cloth, and brown, burgundy, or purple candles. Decorate with bunches of dried herbs, sunflowers, autumn leaves, potatoes, acorns, and Indian corn. Burn Mabon Incense (a mixture of hibiscus, myrrh, rose petals, and sage).

Cast Circle using the athame. After ritual, leave any edible decorations (herbs, sunflowers, acorns, corn, and so on) outdoors for the wildlife to enjoy.

Mabon Celebration Ideas

- Potatoes are very symbolic at Mabon, for they grow and take shape under the ground. For this reason, many Crafters like to have a potato bake during this celebration. Just rake the leaves from your yard, then use them for a bonfire to welcome the fall season. Wrap potatoes in foil, bake them in the fire, and thank the Earth for Her bounty by saying something like:

> *O Goddess Mother of us all*
> *We thank You as Your blessings fall*
> *Upon us—each and every soul—*
> *As the year wheel turns and rolls*
> *For nourishing our bodies and*
> *Our spirits with Your gifts from land*
> *For Your abundance on the Earth*
> *We give you thanks with love and mirth*

- Honor family ancestors with a feast of oatmeal walnut cookies and apple juice. Set a place for everyone present, and include place settings for the honorees. Go through family albums or photographs, recall the life stories of the ancestors pictured, and meditate upon the importance of their lives. Remember how each family member gone before lives on in you. End by thanking the ancestors for the roles they continue to play in your lives by saying something like:

For your lives, I give you thanks
You, who live now in the ranks
Of memories of times now past
Whose blood still flows within me fast
Whose personalities I share
Whose mannerisms here and there
Come out in me from time to time
Bringing reason to my rhyme
I thank you for the parts of me
You've put in place that I might be
I promise now that you shall thrive
With loving thoughts throughout my life
For all I am and all I'll be
Is because you live in me

- Get up early on Mabon morning. Listen to the songbirds in the trees, and bid a fond farewell to those creatures who begin to burrow beneath the Earth for winter hibernation.

- Using a needle, draw pieces of monofilament cord through several sunflowers. Hang the flowers in trees so the birds can eat the seeds. As you hang each flower, say something like:

Symbol of Sun, Who now departs
And leaves the world both cold and dark
Live on within these seeds of Light
And feed our feathered friends in flight
That they may thrive in winter's chill
Until again with light you fill
The Earth and shine again anew
Replacing ice with morning dew

- Remember that thanksgiving isn't just about saying thank you. It also involves giving something back for all you've received in life. That being the case, volunteer at a hospital, or spend some time visiting the elderly. Even better, plan to spend a day working at a soup kitchen or homeless shelter. It will not only lighten the hearts of those you touch, but bring you the blessings of reciprocation. Blessings are much more valuable than anything else we hold!

AFTERWORD

IT'S ALWAYS BEEN MY contention that people are afraid of the Craft not so much because of antiquated stereotypes, but because they simply don't know what it involves. It's the human factor at work. A simple case of fearing the unknown. And when that much fear is involved, minds close and communication channels shut down. The worst part is that no amount of education makes any difference. Fact is, you just can't educate those who don't want to learn. It's a little like begging a child to try a new dish. You can plead, bargain, and threaten. But no matter what you do, they're just not going to take that first bite. Not unless they want to.

Because I found this attitude so ridiculous, I've always done my best to keep an open mind no matter what crossed my path. I've taken pride in it. Congratulated myself. And more than once, even served it up with relish as my best quality. That's why it was so ironic that—as I wrote this book—the Ancients chose to throw me headlong into a sea of change. If They'd just made a few minor alterations, I'd have shrugged my shoulders and gone on. But such wasn't the case. They planned and plotted until They devised a real cesspool. And life as I knew it fell in and drowned. A long-term relationship ended unpleasantly. I left my home. My finances went to hell in a hand basket. And if that weren't enough, my child picked that exact time to move out and join the army. Life dissolved before my very eyes. I kicked and screamed. Bucked and snorted. But none of it did any good. Finally, I just sat back and wondered what I'd done to deserve so much chaos.

Then it hit me. I was guilty of exactly the same thing I'd preached against for so long. Fear of the unknown. Fear for no reason. Fear of trying something new. I was like the child who had no intention whatsoever of taking that first bite. That child who didn't know what she was missing.

So with nothing left to lose, I dipped my spoon into a new day. Reluctantly, I took a big bite. And what I discovered was amazing. There was a side to life I'd never known. It was sweet. Magical. And totally irresistible. It was all I'd ever dreamed of and then some. Looking back now, it's sad to think I could have missed it all.

Here's the point. Change, while not always pleasant, is always imminent. It's an ongoing, important process that powers the world and those who live in it. But for those of us who practice the Ancient Arts, it's even more important. That's because change—even with all its aggravations—is the basis for magic. And when we begin to see it for what it really is, the heart's desire is more than just possible. It becomes a reality so true and so clear that we can literally reach out and touch it.

That being the case, don't delay. Shed your innermost fears and toss them in the trash. Then grab a spoon and dip it deep into the bowl of change. Magic is only one bite away. And it's waiting there just for you!

COMMON DREAM SYMBOLS

Accidents: A change in life status

Airplane: Reach for your goals

Alcohol: Pleasure and wealth

Ancestors: Good news for a far away place

Angel: A long, happy, peaceful life

Ants: The ability to make a great sum of money

Antiques: A well-kept secret will be revealed

Apple: Riches and contentment

Apron: Good health and prosperity

Artist: Pleasure; good fortune in current projects

Baby: Good health and financial success

Bacon: A happy marriage in the near future

Balcony: Happy love affairs

Balloon: A rise in financial status

Barn: Wealth

Bath: Pleasure

Beach: Peace and satisfaction

Beads: Good decisions will bring popularity and wealth

Bees: Fertility and abundance

Bird's Nest: Good luck and happiness

Bottle: Good health through moderation

Bracelet: A new romantic interest

Bridge: The end of problems

Cake: An extreme financial gain

Camp Fire: Good health

Candle: Knowledge; a successful future

Cards: Dreams realized and met with fruition

Cat: Stealth

Cemetery: Shrewd business transactions

Chapel: A prosperous, happy marriage

Clock: Steady, successful employment

Crocodile: An uncovered secret

Cup: Sudden wealth; good luck in matters of the heart

Daisies: Good luck

Dance: Joyous contentment

Diamond: A raise in salary

Dog: A kind and faithful friend

Duck: A trip over water

Eagle: Freedom associated with sudden wealth

Eggs: Success and joy; if broken, slander and jealousy

Elephant: Power, success, and dignity

Envelope: Message by mail; if empty, sad news

Eyes: A great understanding of people

Fairy: Joy and freedom

Fence: Peace and protection

Firefly: True love

Fish: A pregnancy

Flame: A very exciting future

Flying: A successful career

Fog: Protection; the ability to outwit enemies

Frog: An educated, prosperous, prominent family

Garden: A pleasant surprise; happiness and wealth

Gate: Newfound prosperity

Gift: A kind-hearted, gentle, nurturing person

Gold: Goals achieved, but only through personal effort

Grain: Prosperous endeavors

Hat: Wishes granted

Holiday: Watch your spending and don't live above your means

Horse Shoe: Good luck, especially in games of chance

Hummingbird: A personal endeavor will greatly benefit others

Injury: Trouble at work

Island: Loneliness

Jumping: A beneficial move

Kitchen: Peaceful, satisfying life

Lake: General success

Lamp: Power through education

Lion: Strength and courage

Loan: Lost or endangered friendship

Lock: Personal security

Lottery: Gambling luck on the following day

Magic: An increase in power; association with powerful people

Magnet: True love; prosperity

Matches: A friend will have a slight accident

Mice: Quick and easy defeat of enemies

Money: Good fortune, power, and dignity

Moon: Success in love

Moving: A raise in finances

Necklace: Love, joy, and success

Newspaper: A letter or message containing good news

Notebook: Great knowledge and study skills

Oak: A fruitful and long-lasting career

Ocean: Friends need your help

Oranges: Success and good health

Oven: A happy surprise

Package: Success despite difficulty

Paint: Fresh insight; possible change of address

Parade: Good leadership qualities

Peacock: Faulty business decisions

Pills: Loss of confidence in a trusted friend

Post Card: Success and popularity in business

Prison: Loss and sorrow

Quilt: Good health, wealth, and wisdom

Rabbit: Good luck, joy, and profit

Rain: Financial success; garden abundance

Rainbow: Successful life; messages from the spirit world

Rice: Wealth and happiness, especially for gamblers

River: A brilliant future and an honorable career

Road: Success in business and love

Rug: A social event will bring a romantic partner

Sailing: Business security and good health

Scissors: A loving family

Searching: Aggravation and disappointment

Seashore: A reunion with friends or relatives

Shopping: Joy and prosperity

Silk: Happiness and success; you may receive an expensive gift

Song: Happy news; success

Spirits: Pay attention to what's going on around you

Sun: Success and happiness

Swing: Good fortune; a possible change of address

Teacher: A successful career

Telescope: A spy; the discovery of a shocking secret

Thunder: Sad news

Treasure: An inheritance

Umbrella: Protection

Verdict: Shocking news

Victory: Long life and much happiness

Voyage: Hopes will come to fruition shortly

Walking: Minor difficulties in achieving a goal

War: Great disappointment

Warning: Guard your personal affairs

Weeds: Jealousy from neighbors and friends

Whistling: Popularity and successful endeavors

Witch: Pay attention to what she says; heed her advice

Wolf: Dangerous enemies

Yellow: Success in endeavors

Zoo: A gain in experience from a current situation

APPENDIX B

THE MAGICAL USES OF HERBS, PLANTS, FLOWERS, AND TREEES

Anger Management: Almond, Catnip, Chamomile, Elecampane, Rose, Lemon Balm, Lavender, Mint, Passion flower, Vervain

Anxiety Management: Skullcap, Valerian

Apathy: Ginger, Peppermint

Beauty: Avocado, Catnip, Flax, Ginseng, Maidenhair fern, Rose, Rosemary, Witch hazel

Business Success: Basil, Hawthorn, Sandalwood, Squill Root

Courage: Borage, Cedar, Columbine, Masterwort, Mullein, Sweet pea, Thyme, Tonka bean, Yarrow

Depression Management: Catnip, Celandine, Daisy, Hawthorn, Honeysuckle, Hyacinth, Lemon Balm, Lily of the Valley, Marjoram, Morning Glory, Saffron, Sheperd's Purse

Divination: Camphor, Dandelion, Goldenrod, Ground Ivy, Henbane, Hazelnut, Hibiscus, Meadowsweet, Mugwort, Pomegranate

Employment: Bergamot, Bayberry, Bay Leaf, Pecan, Pine

Enemies: Patchouli, Slippery Elm

Friendship: Lemon, Orange, Sunflower, Sweet Pea, Tonka Bean, Vanilla

Gambling: Buckeye, Chamomile, Pine

Gossip Management: Clove, Deerstongue, Nettle, Rue, Slippery Elm, Snapdragon

Health/Healing: Fennel, Flax, Garlic, Ginseng, Golden Seal, Heliotrope, Hops, Horehound, Ivy, Lemon Balm, Life Everlasting, Mint, Mugwort, Myrrh, Nasturtium, Nutmeg, Oak, Olive, Onion, Peppermint, Persimmon, Pine,

Plaintain, Rosemary, Rowan, Rue, Saffron, Sandlewood, Sheperd's Purse, Thistle, Thyme, Vervain, Violet, Willow, Wintergreen, Yerba Santa

Heartbreak Management: Apple, Bittersweet, Cyclamen, Honeysuckle, Jasmine, Lemon Balm, Magnolia, Peach, Strawberry, Yarrow

Hunting: Acorn, Apple, Cypress, Juniper, Mesquite, Oak, Pine, Sage, Vanilla

Legal Matters: Buckthorn, Celandine, Chamomile, Galangal, Hickory, High John, Marigold

Liberation: Chicory, Cypress, Lavender, Lotus, Mistletoe, Moonflower

Love: Adam & Eve Root, Allspice, Apple, Apricot, Balm of Gilead, Basil, Bleeding Heart, Cardamon, Catnip, Chamomile, Cinnamon, Clove, Columbine, Copal, Coriander, Crocus, Cubeb, Daffodil, Daisy, Damiana, Dill, Elecampane, Elm, Endive, Fig, Gardinia, Geranium, Ginger, Hibiscus, Hyacinth, Indian Paintbrush, Jasmine, Juniper, Kava-Kava, Lady's Mantle, Lavender, Lemon Balm, Lemon Verbena, Linden, Lobelia, Lotus, Loveage, Maidenhair Fern, Mandrake, Maple, Marjoram, Myrtle, Nutmeg, Orchid, Pansy, Peach, Peppermint, Periwinkle, Poppy, Primrose, Rose, Rosemary, Rue, Saffron, Skullcap, Spearmint, Spiderwort, Strawberry, Thyme, Tonka Bean, Tulip, Vanilla, Vervain, Violet, Willow, Wood Betony, Yarrow

Luck: Allspice, Anise, Bluebell, Calamus, China Berry, Daffodil, Hazel, Heather, Holly, Job's Tears, Linden, Lucky Hand, Nutmeg, Oak, Orange, Persimmon, Pomegranate, Poppy, Rose, Snakeroot, Vertivert, Violet

Lust: Allspice, Caraway, Carrot, Cattail, Cinnamon, Cinquefoil, Clove, Damiana, Deerstongue, Dill, Foxglove, Galangal, Ginseng, Hibiscus, Mistletoe, Parsley, Rosemary, Sesame, Southernwood, Vanilla, Violet, Yohimbe

Menopause: Black Cohosh, Lavender, Peppermint, Sage

Mental Powers: All Heal, Bay leaf, Caraway, Celery Seed, Forget-Me-Not, Hazel, Horehound, Lily of the Valley, Lotus, Pansy, Periwinkle, Rue, Sandalwood, Spikenard, Summer Savory, Spearmint

Nightmare Prevention: Mullein, Chamomile

PMS: Feverfew, Jasmine, Lavender, Rose

Prophetic Dreams: Anise, Chamomile, Cinquefoil, Cloves, Heliotrope, Jasmine, Mimosa, Mint, Mugwort, Rose, Rosemary, Valerian

Prosperity: Almond, Bay leaf, Basil, Bergamot, Cedar, Chamomile, Cinnamon, Cinquefoil, Clover, Mandrake, Marjoram, May Apple, Myrtle, Oak, Orange Mint, Parsley, Peacan, Pine, Snapdragon, Sunflower, Sweet Woodruff, Tonka Bean, Tulip, Vanilla, Vervain, Wheat

Protection: African Violet, Agrimony, Aloe Vera, Alyssum, Angelica, Anise, Arrowroot, Asafoetida, Balm of Gilead, Basil, Bay Leaf, Birch, Bladderwrack, Boneset, Bromeliad, Broom, Burdock, Cactus, Calamus, Caraway, Carnation, Cedar, Chrysanthemum, Cinnamon, Cinquefoil, Clove, Clover, Cumin, Curry, Cyclamen, Cypress, Datura, Dill, Dogweed, Dragon's Blood, Elder, Elecampane, Eucalyptus, Fennel, Feverwort, Flax, Fleabane, Foxglove, Frankincense, Galangal, Garlic, Geranium, Ginseng, Heather, Holly, Honeysuckle, Horehound, Houseleek, Hyacinth, Hyssop, Ivy, Juniper, Lady's Slipper, Larkspur, Lavender, Lilac, Lily, Linden, Lotus, Lucky Hand, Mallow, Mandrake, Marigold, Mimosa, Mint, Mistletoe Mugwort, Mulberry, Mullein, Mustard, Myrrh, Nettle, Oak, Olive, Onion, Parsley, Pennyroyal, Peony, Pepper, Periwinkle, Pine, Plaintain, Primrose, Quince, Radish, Raspberry, Rattlesnake Root, Rhubarb, Rose, Rowan, Rue, Sage, St. John's Wort, Sandlewood, Snapdragon, Southernwood, Spanish Moss, Sweet Woodruff, Thistle, Tulip, Valerian, Vervain, Violet, Willow, Wintergreen, Witch Hazel, Wolfbane, Wormwood, Wood Betony, Yucca

Psychic Ability: Celery, Cinnamon, Citronella, Elecampane, Eyebright, Flax, Galangal, Honeysuckle, Lemongrass, Mace, Marigold, Mugwort, Peppermint, Rose, Rowan, Star Anise, Thyme, Uva Ursa, Wormwood, Yarrow

Sexual Harassment Management: Bergamot, Camphor, Salt Petre, Vervain, Witch Hazel

Sleep: Agrimony, Chamomile, Cinquefoil, Elder, Hops, Lavender, Linden, Peppermint, Rosemary, Sheperd's Purse, Thyme, Valerian, Vervain

Strength: Acorn, Bay Leaf, Carnation, Mugwort, Mulberry, Pennyroyal, Plaintain, St. John's Wort, Thistle

Stress Management: Calandula, Chamomile, Comfrey, Hops, Lavender, Nettle, Oats, St. John's Wort, Passion Flower, Skullcap

Success: Cinnamon, Clover, Ginger, High John, Lemon Balm, Orange, Rowan

Theft: Caraway, Elder, Garlic, Gentian, Juniper, Rosemary, Vertivert

Travel: Blatterwrack, Lavender

Victory: Bay Leaf, High John, Olive

Wisdom: Hazel, Rowan, Sage, Spikenard

Wishes: Bay Leaf, Dandelion, Dogwood, Hazel, Job's Tears, Sage, Sunflower, Tonka Bean, Vanilla, Vervain, Violet, Walnut

THE MAGICAL USES OF STONES

Amplification: Orange Calcite, Quartz Crystal

Anger Management: Amethyst, Carnelian, Lepidolite, Topaz

Beauty: Amber, Cat's Eye, Jasper, Opal, Rose Quartz, Unakite

Business Success: Green Agate, Aventurine, Bloodstone, Emerald, Jade, Lapis Lazuli, Malachite, Green Tourmaline

Change: Ametrine, Opal, Unakite, Watermelon Tourmaline

Childbirth: Geode, Moonstone, Mother-of-Pearl

Cleansing: Aquamarine, Salt

Courage: Agate, Amethyst, Aquamarine, Bloodstone, Carnelian, Diamond, Hematite, Lapiz Lazuli, Tiger-Eye, Watermelon Tourmaline, Turquoise

Creativity: Orange Calcite, Citrine, Opal, Topaz

Depression Management: Blue Agate, Kunzite

Dieting: Moonstone, Blue Topaz

Divination: Amethyst, Azurite, Hematite, Moonstone, Rainbow Obsidian, Opal, Quartz Crystal

Dreams: Amethyst, Azurite, Citrine, Opal, Snowflake Obsidian

Eloquence: Carnelian, Celestite, Emerald

Friendship: Chrysoprase, Rose Quartz, Pink Tourmaline, Turquoise

Gambling: Amazonite, Aventurine, Tiger-Eye

Gardening: Green Agate, Moss Agate, Jade, Malachite, Quartz Crystal

Grounding: Hematite, Kunzite, Moonstone, Obsidian, Salt, Black Tourmaline

Bad Habit Management: Moonstone, Obsidian, Black Onyx

Healing/Health: Green Agate, Banded Agate, Amethyst, Aventurine, Azurite, Bloodstone, Carnelian, Chrysoprase, Coral, Diamond, Flint, Garnet, Hematite, Holey Stones, Jade, Jasper, Lapis Lazuli, Peridot, Petrified Wood, Quartz Crystal, Smoky Quartz, Sapphire, Sodalite, Staurolite, Sugilite, Sunstone, Yellow Topaz, Turquoise

Joy: Orange Calcite, Chrysoprase, Sunstone, Unakite

Love: Alexandrite, Amber, Amethyst, Chrysocolla, Diamond, Emerald, Jade, Laps Lazuli, Lepidolite, Malachite, Moonstone, Opal, Pearl, Rose Quartz, Rhodocrosite, Sapphire, Topaz, Pink Tourmaline, Turquoise

Luck: Alexandrite, Amber, Apache Tear, Aventurine, Chalcedony, Chrysoprase, Holey Stones, Lepidolite, Opal, Pearl, Tiger-Eye, Turquoise

Lust: Carnelian, Coral, Sunstone, Mahogany Obsidian

Magical Power: Bloodstone, Orange Calcite, Quartz Crystal, Malachite, Opal, Ruby

Meditation: Ametrine, Geodes, Hematite, Quartz Crystal, Sodalite, Sugilite

Mental Ability: Aventurine, Citrine, Emerald, Flourite, Quartz Crystal

Nightmare Prevention: Chalcedony, Citrine, Holey Stones, Lepidolite, Ruby

Peace: Blue Agate, Amethyst, Aquamarine, Aventurine, Carnelian, Chalcedony, Chrysocolla, Coral, Diamond, Kunzite, Lepidolite, Malachite, Obsidian, Rhodocrosite, Rodonite, Sapphire, Sodalite, Blue Tourmaline

Peaceful Separation: Black Onyx, Black Tourmaline

Physical Energy: Banded Agate, Garnet, Quartz Crystal, Rhodocrosite, Sunstone, Tiger-Eye

Physical Strength: Banded Agate, Amber, Bloodstone, Diamond, Garnet, Cubic Zirconia

Prosperity: Abalone, Green Agate, Aventurine, Bloodstone, Chrysoprase, Emerald, Jade, Mother-of-Pearl, Malachite, Opal, Pearl, Peridot, Ruby, Sapphire, Staurolite, Tiger-Eye, Green Tourmaline

Protection: Apache Tear, Carnelian, Chalcedony, Chrysoprase, Citrine, Coral, Diamond, Emerald, Flint, Garnet, Holey Stones, Jade, Jasper, Lapis Lazuli, Lepidolite, Malachite, Marble, Moonstone, Mother-of-Pearl, Obsidian, Pearl, Peridot, Petrified Wood, Quartz Crystal, Ruby, Salt, Staurolite, Sunstone, Tiger-Eye, Smoky Topaz, Black Tourmaline, Turquoise

Psychic Ability: Amethyst, Aquamarine, Azurite, Citrine, Quartz Crystal, Emerald, Holey Stones, Lapis Lazuli

Psychic Attack Management: Alexandrite, Flourite, Hematite, Opal

Spirituality: Amethyst, Lepidolite, Sodalite, Sugilite

Stress Management: Amethyst, Chrysoprase, Leopard Skin Agate, Jade, Brecciated Jasper, Paua Shell

Success: Amazonite, Chrysoprase, Marble

Theft Management: Garnet, Cubic Zirconia

Travel: Aquamarine, Chalcedony

Wisdom: Amethyst, Chrysocolla, Coral, Jade, Sodalite, Sugilite

DEITY ASSOCIATIONS

FOR FURTHER INFORMATION ON Deity origin and history, please check the internet or local public library. *(Note:* genders are abbreviated for convenience.)

Business: Athena (F), Ebisu (M), Gaia (F), Jupiter (M), Midas (M)

Change: Bloedewydd (F), Brighid (F), Cerridwyn (F), Epona (F), Nemesis (F), Persephone (F), Rhiannon (F), Spider Woman (F), Vertumnus (M)

Childbirth: Aphrodite (F), Arianrhod (F), Brighid (F), Demeter (F), Gaia (F), Hera (F), Ilmatar (F)

Communication: Amerigin (M), Baduh (M), Bharati (F), Brighid (F), Gadel (M), Hashye-Atlye (M), Hermes (M), Hu (M), Ikto (M), Imaluris (M), Iris (F), Nabu (M), Oghma (M), Pairikas (F), Sarasvati (F)

Computers and Peripherals: Loki (M), Murphy (M), Thor (M), Zeus (M)

Modem: Hermes (M), Mercury (M), Sarasvati (F)

Scanner: Brighid (F), Venus (F)

Courage: Achilles (M), Apollo (M), Ares (M), Artemis (F), Athene (F), Atlas (M), Bellora (F), Diana (F), Hercules (M), Mars (M), Morgan (F), Neith (F), Persephone (F), Perseus (M)

Creativity: Apollo (M), Artemis Calliste (F), Athena (F), Bragi (M), Brighid (F), Ilmatar (F), Odin (M), Maya (F), Minerva (F), the Muses (F), Namagiri (F), Ptah (M), Tvashtri (M), Veveteotl (M), Wayland (M)

Divination: Adrste (F), Ashtoreth (F), Bannik (M), Carmenta (F), Dione (F), Egeria (F), Evander (M), Filia Vocis (F), Gaia (F), Gwendydd (F), Inanna (F), Kwan Yin (F), Mari (F), Namagiri (F), Odin (M), Shamash (M), Thoth (M)

Fertility: Acat (M), Ahurani (F), Aima, (F), Althea (F), Amahita (F), Anat (F), Apollo (M), Arianrhod (F), Astarte (F), Atergatis (F), Baal (M), Baccus (M), Berchta (F), Bona Dea (F), Brimo (F), Ceres (F), Cupra (F), Damara (F), Demeter (F), Dionysus (M), Fortuna (F), Freya (F), Lono (F), Ma (F), Neith (F), Rhea (F), Wajwer (M)

Friendship: Hathor (F), Maitri (F), Mithras (M)

Gardening: Ceres (F), Rhea (F), Theano (F)

Gossip: Tacita (F)

Harmony: Alcyone (F), Concordia (F), Forseti (M), Harmonia (F), Kuan-Ti (M), Pax (F)

Healing/Health: Aphrodite (F), Apollo (M), Artemis (F), Asclepius (M), Brighid (F), Ceadda (M), Diancecht (M), Eir (F), Esculapius (M), Gula (F), Hygeia (F), Karusepas (F), Kedesh (F), Kwan Yin (F), Liban (F), Meditrina (F), Rhiannon (F), Salus (F), Tien Kuan (M)

Heartbreak: Apollo (M), Diana (F), Gaia (F), Luna (F), Selena (F)

Home: Bannik (M), Cardea (F), Da-Bog (M), Dugnai (F), Gucumatz (M), Hastehogan (M), Hestia (F), Kikimora (F), Neith (F), the Lares (M), Penates (M), Vesta (F)

Hunting: Apollo (M), Artemis (F), Diana (F), Vali (M), Ydalir (M)

Joy: Amaterasu (F), Ataksak (M), Baldur, Fu-Hsing (M), Hathor (F), Hotei (M), Omacatl (M), Samkhat (F), Tien Kuan (M)

Justice: Aleitheia (F), Anase (M), Apollo (M), Astraea (F), Athene (F), Forseti (M), Hecate (F), Justita (F), Ida-Ten (M), Kali (F), Ma'at (F), Mens (F), Misharu (M), Mithras (M), the Morrigan (F), Musku (M), Syn (F), Tyr (M), Varuna (M)

Knowledge: Gwion (M), Hanuman (M), Hecate (F), Hermes (M), K'uei Hsing (M), Lugh (M), Ormazd (M), Minerva (F), Mnemosyne (F), Shing Mu (F), Sia (M), Tenjin (M), Toma (F)

Liberation: Artemis (F), Carna (F), Diana (F), Libertas (F), Liberty (F), Terminus (F)

Lightning: Agni (M), Thor (M), Thunor (M), Tien Mu (F)

Love: Amun Ra (M), Anat (F), Angus (M), Aphrodite (F), Astarte (F), Belili (F), Belit-Ilanit (F), Benten (F), Cupid (M), Cybele (F), Erzulie (F), Hathor (F), Ishtar (F), Isis (F), Kama (M), Venus (F)

Luck: Agathadaimon (M), Benten (F), Bonus Eventus (M), Buddha (M), Chala (F), Diakoku (M), Felicitas (F), Fortuna (F), Gansea (M), Kichijo-Ten (F), Lakshmi (F), Muses, The, (F), Tamon (M)

Lunar Workings: Al-lat (F), Anumati (F), Artemis (F), Ashima (F), Belili (F), Callisto (F), Diana (F), Fati (M), Gou (M), Iah (M), Ilmagah (M), Jerah (F), Levanah (F), Luna (F), Mah (M), Mani (M), Re (F), Selene (F)

Lust: Aphrodite (F), Arami (F), Bes (M), Eros (M), Hathor (F), Heket (F), Indrani (F), Isis (F), Ishtar (F), Lalita (F), Lilith (F), Min (M), Pan (M), Rati (F), Venus (F), Yarilo (M)

Magical Power: AMathaon (M), Aradia (F), Ayizan (F), Cernunnos (M), Cerridwen (F), Circe (F), Dakinis (F), Demeter (F), Diana (F), Ea (M), Eterna (M), Gulleig (F), Habondia (F), Hecate (F), Herodias (F), Holle (F), Kwan Yin (F), Mari (F), Odin (M), Rangda (F), Thoth (M), Untunktahe (M)

Marriage: Aramati (F), Fides (F), Gaia (F), Hera (F), Ida (F)

New Endeavors: Amun Ra (M), Apollo (M), Brighid (F), Cerridwen (F), Iris (F), Janus (M), Laurentina (F), Muses, The (F)

Obstacles: Atlas (M), Carna (F), Janus (M), Lilith (F), Syn (F), Terminus (M)

Opportunity: Brighid (F), Carna (F), Janus (M), Syn (F)

Pets: Bast (F), Diana (F), Melusine (F), Pan (M), Rhea (F), Rhiannon (F)

Power: Atlas (M), Athena (F), Kali (F), Minerva (F), Zeus (M)

Prosperity: Anna Koun (F), Anna Perenna (F), Benten (F), Buddhi (F), Daikoku (M), Inari (M), Jambhala (M), Jupiter (M), Lakshmi (F), Ops (F), Pluto (M), Vasudhara (F)

Protection: Aditi (F), Ares (M), Atar (M), Athena (M), Auchimalgen (F), Eris (F), Hecate (F), Kali (F), Mars (M), Nahmauit (F), Padmapani (M), Prometheus (M), Sheila-na-gig (F), Shiu-Kuan (M), Syen (M), Thor (M), Zeus (M)

Psychic Ability: Apollo (M), Hecate (F), Odin (M), Psyche (F), Rowana (F), Thoth (M)

Rain: Agni (M), Gwalu (M), Mama Quilla (F), Melusine (F), Sadwes (F), Tallai (F)

Snow: Father Winter (M), Holle (F), Kriss Kringle (M)

Solar Workings: Amaterasu (F), Amun Ra (M), Apollo (M), Aya (F), Asva (F), Baldur (M), Bast (F), Bochica (M), Da-Bog (M), Dyaus (M), Eos (F), Helios (M), Hsi-Ho (F), Hyperion (M), Igaehindvo (F), Li (F), Maui (M), Sul (F), Sunna (F), Sunniva (F), Surya (M)

Storms: Hadad (M), Rodasi (F), Tempestus (F)

Strength: Achilles (M), Atlas (M), Hercules (M), Thor (M), Zeus (M)

Success: Anu (F), Apollo (M), Diana (F), Fortuna (F)

Thunder: Peroun (M), Zeus (M)

Travel: Beielbog (M), Ekchuah (M), Hasammelis (M), Kunado (M), Mercury (M)

Victory: Hercules (M), Korraual (F), Nike (F), Pallus Athena (F), Vijaya (F), Victoria (F)

War: Ares (M), Athena (F), Eris (F), Mars (M), Thor (M)

Wind: Aeolus (M), Awhiowhio (M), Boreas (M), Oya (F), Sarama (F)

Wisdom: Athena (F), Atri (M), Baldur (M), Bragi (M), Buddha (M), Dainichi (M), Demeter (F), Diana (F), Ea (M), Ekadzati (F), Gasmu (F), Heh (F), Metis (F), Minerva (F), Namagiri (F), Oannes (M), Persephone (F), Prajna (F), Sapientia (F), Shekinah (F), Sophia (F), Thoth (F), Victoria (F)

THE BOOK OF LAW

WHEN THE CRAFT WAS new, it needed a bit of structure—just a little something to hold it together. For that reason, the Elders wrote a Book of Law—a set of tenets, if you will—for practicing the Craft in peace and harmony. While we don't often find practical application of these laws today, they are still excellent guidelines, and provide a good historical reference of our Craft.

For your convenience, I've divided it into two sections: laws that once applied to all Wiccans, and those that applied more to the Craft when practiced in a group or coven.

Section 1

1. Love the Gods and honor Them, for They are the matrix from which the Life Force springs. Remember that this Force courses through the veins of all living beings. For that reason, treat yourself and those around you as well as you treat the Gods, and the Gods, in turn, will love and honor you.

2. We are the children of the Lord and the Lady, Who rule the Universe and all that is held within its boundaries. Treat Them with parental respect and do not test Them, for They are not to be trifled with.

3. Only use the Craft in love, so that the energy you create becomes a beacon of light by which to find the Gods. When the Craft is used otherwise, it becomes the net by which you are eventually snared and entangled.

4. Let the Craft unite the children of the Gods to tend the earth and care for its beings.

5. Do not glean the land when working it. Give the fallen fruits, instead, back to the Earth Mother.

6. Be proud of the Wiccan ways, but be ever-mindful not to slip into a pool of vanity. Once you fall in, it's difficult to find your way back into the portal.

7. Speak little and listen much. Reserve judgment until all the facts are in.

8. Be joyful and happy; only then will your life be filled with love.

9. While your teachers serve the Gods by giving the seeds of knowledge, it is up to you to sow them and tend them through harvest. Thus, you reap what you sow. Remember that deceit and misuse of power is cause for karmic retribution.

10. Do not gossip about fellow members of the Craft or hold any malice against them.

11. Do not lie, for what you say in the presence of the Gods becomes manifest in reality.

12. Be nonjudgmental of those who do not embrace the Craft; likewise, do not disclose the identity of anyone who has.

13. Keep your word to fellow members of the Craft, for such is an oath to the Gods.

14. Because the Lord and Lady do not want Their children to suffer oppression or indignity on Their account, They will seek recourse to rectify the matter.

15. Never use the Craft to do harm; in doing so, you bring harm to yourself.

16. Never betray your siblings in the Craft; rather, embrace the virtues of love, honor, and wisdom.

17. Never speak with your mouth that which is not in your heart.

18. Never speak ill of the Gods, for doing so will incur Their anger.

19. Because no one must endanger the Craft, all members must follow the law of the land.

20. Do not haggle over price when obtaining magical tools. To do so cheapens them in the eyes of the Gods.

21. Never accept money for performing spells for others.

22. Never steal. Doing so will cause you to sacrifice something dear to regain Universal balance.

23. Honor all people and respect them; let their eyes reflect your soul.

24. Never accept the pledge of anyone's life, no matter how deeply she or he is indebted to you. To do so is personally burdensome, and will hinder your progress in the Craft.

25. Remember the Law of Karma, and that everything returns to you threefold.

26. Cleanse and bless everything that is brought into the Circle or temple area. This gives honor to the Gods.

27. Honor the Goddess by keeping your house, body, and clothing clean.

28. Remember that no one should die without dignity, love, and respect. Act accordingly.

29. No man or woman should come together in sexual union if it causes pain to another to do so.

30. Let those who would love and bear children be handfasted.

31. Only marry or handfast for love. It is an abomination against the Goddess to do otherwise.

32. Teach and guide your children with love, and remember that they are spawned of the Goddess.

33. It is up to the children of the Gods to maintain their personal strands in the Cosmic Web; in doing so, they allow the Universe to flux and flex when necessary.

34. Respect your power, your magic, and the ways of Wicca. Know that everyone who crosses your path—even if only for a moment—is there to teach you something.

35. Stay physically and mentally fit, for only then will the power in you remain pure.

36. The Circle should always be a fitting place to invite the Gods. For that reason, always purify it as well as those who choose to enter.

37. Remember the message of the Goddess: "I shall not carry you nor hinder you, nor keep you from having the same opportunities as My other children. You are free, and shall not be coddled like babes in a storm. If you have true devotion and desire within you, then any obstacle shall be overcome."

38. Make a sanctuary to the Gods, and only place the purest of energy within.

39. To gain the blessing of the Goddess, make an altar from stone or wood, and light candles and incense in Her honor.

40. Set aside one day during each Moon to do the Lady's work; She shall renew and bless you in return.

41. Study the arts of Circle-casting and ritual with a pure heart and learn them well. Only then will you be a person of power.

42. Each member of the Craft should keep a personal Book of Shadows, detailing the Old Ways and recording their progress.

43. Study the legends of the Gods. They will honor you with Their blessings.

44. If any member of the Craft works within his or her Craft (performs readings or such for others), it is only right that they have just financial compensation.

45. Those who sacrifice some personal pleasure for the good of all shall be remembered and blessed by the Gods.

46. Make offerings of labor and natural gifts to the Gods. Know that you will be blessed accordingly.

47. When you make offerings to restore balance, make sure that your gifts are not offensive to the Gods.

48. Offerings to the Gods made during ritual shall be buried in the earth or burned, in order to return them to the Source from which they sprang.

49. Use the Craft to help yourself, but only in such a way that harm comes to no one.

50. Protect the Craft and all who embrace it, so we may never again fear the Burning Times.

51. The Lady brings us joy and the Lord gifts us with pleasure. Worship in love and enjoy the gifts of both.

52. To preserve the way of the Craft, silence and secrecy are necessary when dealing with those who may wish to harm it.

53. For the continuance of the Craft and its ways, we must work toward achieving both mundane and spiritual balance, and do so with the power of love.

54. Educate those who want to learn, but let love and wisdom be your guide. In this way, the rites of the Craft are kept sacred.

55. No one may enter the Circle if they are physically ill.

56. If a member of the Craft is in need of a house or land, the Craft may be used to expedite such matters provided that it harms none; however, the full price must be paid without haggling.

57. Do not turn any away who seek the Gods. Help them, instead, in their quest.

58. Educate those whose hearts are true and their intentions honest.

59. All students of the Craft must strive to achieve harmony within themselves.

Section 2: Working within a Coven

60. The Circle is the dwelling of the Gods on earth, belongs to their children, and each Circle cast forms a special family. Take care not to cause harm to any Circle family; in doing so, you insult the Gods and do harm to yourself.

61. In disputes involving Circle families, only a tribunal of the Elders may pass judgment.

62. Guests in Circle are to be treated as part of the Craft community.

63. Members of the Craft who do not wish to work toward learning the ancient ways shall be turned away from the temple.

64. Secure and guard any land, money, or property that belongs to the Circle family.

65. A gift given to the Circle or to the Priest/ess is a gift given to honor the Goddess.

66. The Craft may be used to prevent others from harming the Craft or its children, but only after consultation with the members of the Circle and an agreement made between them.

67. The Priestess shall rule the Circle with justice and love.

68. Although the Priest is the Force that builds the Circle, remember that the Priestess rules its realm.

69. The Priestess shall settle all differences within the Circle family, and do so using common sense and justice.

70. Each Circle family may decide whether it should worship in secret or hold open rituals, for only they truly know what dangers lurk in their area.

71. All ritual items should be blessed and dedicated to the Gods, and the Priest and Priestess shall maintain them.

72. Members of the Craft are at liberty to join any Circle family they wish—or form a new one—but only after sharing their intentions with the Priestess and Elders.

73. Circle families may meet to celebrate joint rituals, but must do so in absolute peace and harmony.

74. The Priestess shall mediate quarrels between members of the Circle family, hearing both sides privately, and then together. She shall settle the matter with fairness and love. If no agreement can be reached, however, then one member must leave the Circle family.

75. Those guilty of wrongdoing without knowledge are held innocent; those guilty of wrongdoing by reckless behavior will be dealt with according to the nature of the offense; those guilty of intentional wrongdoing shall be punished threefold by the Priestess and the Elders.

76. Teachers of the Craft must possess the virtues of ability, belief, faith, humility, knowledge, leadership, and patience, and possess a loving nature.

77. Accept the advice of the Priest and Priestess, question wisely, then weigh their wisdom.

78. Should ill health strike the Priest or Priestess, let them step aside until physical vitality is restored.

79. Should a Priest or Priestess grow weary of their duties, they may step down— but only after training someone to fill their position.

80. Any Priest, Priestess, or Elder who condones a breach of the laws must step down from their position.

81. The Priestess may take a leave of absence from office for a year and a day. The Maiden shall resume her duties during that time. Should the Priestess not return within that time limit, then the Maiden shall become Priestess of the Circle family.

82. Priests and Priestesses shall set priorities so as not to neglect their mates or families, nor the sick or needy of the Circle family.

83. The Priestess must remember to give the Priest due respect, for even though the Life Force springs from her, he is the catalyst of that force.

MAIL ORDER SUPPLY STORES

Herbs and Arts
2015 E. Colfax Avenue
Denver, CO 80206
Phone: 303-388-2544
www.herbsnarts.com

Lady Sprite's Cupboard
3184 E. Indian School Rd.
Phoenix, AZ 85016
Phone: 602-956-3539
www.ladyspritescupboard.com

Pathways
8980 Watson Road
St. Louis, MO 63119
Phone: 314-842-0047
www.pathwaysstl.com

Points of Light
4358 Stearns Street
Long Beach, CA 90815
Phone: 562-985-3388
www.pointsoflight.com

Salem West
1209 North High Street
Columbus, OH 43201
Phone: 614-421-7557
www.neopagan.com

Soul Journey
9 Main Street
Butler, NJ 07405
Phone: 973-838-6564
www.souljourney.com

SUGGESTED READING LIST

WHILE THIS VOLUME WAS written mostly from my own experience and studies within the Craft, please understand that I am not the "end-all-and-be-all" of magical knowledge. Others have much to teach, and the following books may prove helpful in your quest for further study.

Beyerl, Paul. *Master Book of Herbalism*. Custer, Wash.: Phoenix Publishing, 1984.

Buckland, Raymond. *Buckland's Complete Book of Witchcraft*. St. Paul, Minn.: Llewellyn Publications, 1986.

Cunningham, Scott. *Cunningham's Encyclopedia of Crystal, Gem and Metal Magic*. St. Paul, Minn.: Llewellyn Publications, 1987.

————. *Cunningham's Encyclopedia of Magical Herbs*. St. Paul, Minn.: Llewellyn Publications, 1986.

————. *The Complete Book of Oils, Incenses, and Brews*. St. Paul, Minn.: Llewellyn Publications, 1989.

David, Judithann H., Ph.D. *Michael's Gemstone Dictionary*. Channeled by J. P. Van Hulle. Orinda, Calif.: The Michael Educational Foundation and Affinity Press, 1986.

Drew, A. J. *Wicca For Men*. Secaucus, N.J.: Carol Publishing Group, 1998.

Fitch, Ed. *Magical Rites From The Crystal Well*. St. Paul, Minn.: Llewellyn Publications, 1989.

Hamilton, Edith. *Mythology: Timeless Tales of Gods and Heroes*. New York, N.Y.: Mentor Books, 1940.

Kerenyi, Karl. *Goddesses of Sun and Moon*. Translated from German by Murray Stein. Dallas, Tex.: Spring Publications, Inc., 1979.

Kunz, George Frederick. *The Curious Lore of Precious Stones*. Copyright 1913 by J. B. Lippincott Company, Philadelphia, Penn.; copyright renewed 1941 by Ruby Kunz Zinsser; published 1971 by Dover Publications, Inc., New York, N.Y., by special arrangement with J. P. Lippincott Company.

Malbrough, Ray T. *Charms, Spells & Formulas*. St. Paul, Minn.: Llewellyn Publications, 1986.

Medici, Marina. *Good Magic*. London, England: Mcmillan London Limited, 1988. New York, N.Y.: Prentice Hall Press, a Division of Simon & Schuster Inc., 1989.

Melody. *Love is in the Earth: A Kaleidoscope of Crystals*. Wheat Ridge, Colo.: Earth-Love Publishing House, 1995.

Monoghan, Patricia. *The New Book of Goddesses and Heroines*. St. Paul, Minn.: Llewellyn Publications, 1997.

———. *The Goddess Path*. St. Paul, Minn.: Llewellyn Publications, 1999.

Morrison, Dorothy. *Everyday Magic: Spells and Rituals for Modern Living*. St. Paul, Minn.: Llewellyn Publications, 1998.

Morrison, Sarah Lyddon. *The Modern Witch's Spellbook*. Secaucus, N.J.: Citadel Press, a Division of Lyle Stuart, Inc., 1971.

Ravenwolf, Silver. *To Ride a Silver Broomstick*. St. Paul, Minn.: Llewellyn Publications, 1994.

Riva, Anna. *The Modern Herbal Spellbook: The Magical Uses of Herbs*. Toluca Lake, Calif.: International Imports, 1974.

Slater, Herman. *The Magickal Formulary*. New York, N.Y.: Magickal Childe Inc., 1981.

Starhawk. *The Spiral Dance: A Rebirth of the Ancient Religion of the Great Goddess*. New York, N.Y.: Harper & Row Publishers, Inc., 1979.

Stone, Merlin. *Ancient Mirrors of Womanhood*. Boston, Mass.: Beacon Press, 1979.

Tarostar. *The Witch's Spellcraft*. Toluca Lake, Calif.: International Imports, 1986.

Telesco, Patricia. *Magick Made Easy.* New York, N.Y.: HarperSanFrancisco, a division of Harper Collins Publishers, 1999.

————. *Spinning Spells, Weaving Wonders.* Freedom, Calif.: Crossing Press, 1996.

Valiente, Doreen. *An ABC of Witchcraft Past and Present.* Custer, Wash.: Phoenix Publishing, 1973.

Walker, Barbara G. *The Woman's Encyclopedia of Myths and Secrets.* New York, N.Y.: Harper & Rowe Publishers, Inc., 1983.

Weinstein, Marion. *Positive Magic.* Custer, Wash.: Phoenix Publishing, 1981.

INDEX

Afternoon, 17

Air, 3, 20, 22–27, 36, 40, 45, 57, 62, 68, 78, 80, 99–100, 103, 112–115, 117–118, 123, 139, 143

Akasha, 26–28, 35, 91, 112–113

Altar, 29, 34–35, 45, 53, 83, 111, 113–115, 118, 120–121, 125, 135–136, 139–140, 142–145, 148, 150, 155, 159, 161, 164, 167, 169, 172–173, 175, 200

Apple Wreath, 135

Athame, 75–82, 87–89, 91, 94–95, 120, 136, 155–156, 159, 172, 175

Banishing, 80, 123, 156

Barley, 145

Beltane, 8, 127, 138, 153, 165–167

Besom, 91, 93, 162

Black Mirror, 91, 93–94

Blood, 63, 72, 76–77, 145, 147–148, 174, 176, 187

Book of Law, The,197

Casting, 75, 109, 116, 124, 136, 154, 162

Cauldron, 7, 53, 91–93, 146, 157, 163, 170

Charge of the God, 14–15, 132

Charge of the Goddess, 14, 132

Chaste, 137

Circle, 7, 14, 20, 58–59, 65, 69, 75, 80, 83–84, 87, 91, 93, 107, 109–125, 129, 133, 135–141, 144–145, 148–150, 154–156, 159, 161–164, 167, 169–170, 172, 175, 199, 201–203, 221

Color, 20–23, 26, 32–36, 47, 55, 57, 69, 73, 75, 83, 89, 164, 215

Corn Dolly, 161, 173

Couplets, 18–19

Cup, 41, 61, 65, 69–73, 77, 87–88, 91–92, 94, 103, 120–121, 180

Dark, 16–17, 26, 34, 62, 76, 79, 92, 123, 131, 149, 151, 157, 167, 174, 176, 217

Days of the Week, 30

Dream Diary, 102

Dyad, 140

Earth, 5, 9, 12, 15, 20, 23–26, 28, 34, 45, 47, 62–63, 68, 79, 83–84, 86, 112, 115, 118–119, 121–122, 125, 134, 136, 138–140, 145–147, 149–150, 154–155, 157–159,

161–163, 165–168, 170–176, 197, 200–201, 208, 219

East, 22, 37–38, 57, 80, 112–114, 117, 122, 124, 168

Elements, 13, 20–28, 46, 84–85, 91, 112–113, 115, 117, 122, 124, 129

Esbat, 127, 131–132, 151

Fire, 5, 14, 16, 20–27, 32, 35, 53, 62, 68, 75, 77–78, 91, 112–113, 115–116, 125, 134, 138, 161, 165–167, 170, 172, 175, 180

Flowers, 14, 25, 42–43, 45–46, 112, 137, 139–140, 142, 164, 166–167, 169, 176, 185, 218

Full, 1, 14, 16–17, 24–25, 43, 59, 61–62, 72, 85, 89, 104, 116, 124, 131–133, 135–149, 151, 154, 201, 215, 220

Hare, 139

Herbs, 39–43, 47, 49, 77, 86, 92–93, 95, 110, 143–144, 146, 154, 158, 161, 163, 165, 168–172, 174–175, 185, 205, 207–208, 216, 218

Imbolc, 93, 127, 153, 160–162, 173

Incense, 24, 40, 47, 62, 77, 92, 113–115, 133, 135–136, 138–140, 142, 144–146, 148–149, 151, 155, 159, 161, 164, 167, 169, 172, 175, 200

Invoking, 34–36, 80, 95, 113, 117–118, 155, 165

Karmic Law, 5, 68

Lammas, 127, 153, 171–172, 174

Large, 9, 26, 30, 33, 41, 45, 47–48, 50, 55, 58–59, 61, 64, 87, 93, 147, 167, 218, 220

Libation, 120–121, 124–125, 133, 135–138, 140–142, 144–146, 148, 158, 162–164

Mabon, 127, 153, 174–176

Mead, 141–142

Meditation, 92–93, 98–99, 110, 142, 190

Midsummer, 127, 153, 168–169

Moon, 5, 7, 9, 13, 16–17, 21, 25, 31, 43, 59, 61–63, 69–70, 72–73, 77, 92, 95, 107, 118, 121, 125, 129, 131–149, 151, 182, 200, 207, 215–221

Moon Phase, 131

Morning, 17, 103, 110, 168, 176, 185

Noon, 17

North, 23, 38–39, 80, 83, 112–114, 118, 123–124, 205

Oak, 16, 46, 132–133, 158–160, 170, 182, 185–187

Ostara, 127, 153, 163–164

Pentacle, 83–89, 91, 95

Pentagram, 45, 83–85, 87–88, 95, 111, 113, 117–118, 123, 155–156

Prayer to the Elements, 27

Quarter Guardians, 112, 122, 125

Rede of the Wicca, 7

Ritual, 4, 14–15, 17–18, 20, 40, 55, 62–63, 69–70, 72, 76, 83–86, 91–95, 97, 110, 113–114, 117, 119–121, 125, 129, 132, 147, 151, 154–155, 157, 159–160, 163–167, 175, 200, 202, 218–221

Ritual Bath, 110, 125

Sabbat, 153, 219

Samhain, 127, 153–155, 157

Seed, 14–15, 30, 77, 119–120, 122, 135, 138, 149, 171, 174, 186

Small, 41, 43, 58–59, 61–62, 64–65, 71, 77–78, 93, 101, 111–113, 116, 139, 143, 147, 155, 162–164, 167, 172–173

Snow, 22, 136–138, 149, 196

South, 7, 21, 37–38, 75, 80, 112–115, 117, 123

Stones, 5, 17, 47–51, 61–62, 79, 112, 154, 158, 161, 163, 165, 168, 171, 174, 189–191, 208, 218–219

Storm, 16, 38, 46, 101, 136, 200

Sun, 5, 13–15, 17, 31, 37, 107, 119–120, 122, 125, 127, 133–134, 138, 140–141, 143, 157–160, 163–174, 176, 183, 207

Sunrise, 17

Sunset, 18, 165

Symbols, 36–37, 45, 61, 68, 84, 103, 113, 117, 133, 136, 163, 170, 179

Thirteen Principles of Wiccan Belief, 9

Tool Consecration Ritual, 63

Transformation Charm, 143

Trees, 45, 47, 140, 159, 170, 176, 218

Wand, 57–69, 75, 91, 93, 113, 116–118, 122–124, 136–137, 159, 162, 164, 167, 169

Waning, 17, 77, 95, 131, 133, 151

Watchtowers, 112, 125

Water, 20–27, 34, 41, 43, 46, 49, 61–63, 68–69, 72–73, 77–79, 92, 94, 110, 112–113, 115, 137, 140–141, 148, 150, 180

Waxing, 7, 16, 43, 131, 151

West, 21, 38, 69, 80, 112–114, 117, 123, 205

White-handled Knife, 91, 95

Wind, 7, 23, 38–39, 48, 71, 77, 98, 116, 120, 196

Wine, 46, 84, 113, 120–121, 124–125, 133, 140, 146–148, 164

Witches Bottle, 173

Witches Creed, 8

Witches Ladder, 142

Wolf, 134–135, 184

Working, 5, 13–30, 33, 60, 65, 71, 76, 83–84, 86–87, 93, 95, 100–103, 105, 122, 135, 144, 165, 169, 176, 197, 201, 221

Wort, 143–145, 168, 170, 187

Yule, 8, 127, 153, 157–160, 163, 172, 217

Yule Log, 159–160

REACH FOR THE MOON

*Llewellyn publishes hundreds of books on your favorite subjects! To get
these exciting books, including the ones on the following pages,
check your local bookstore or order them directly from Llewellyn.*

Order by Phone
- Call toll-free within the U.S. and Canada, 1-800-THE MOON
- In Minnesota, call (651) 291-1970
- We accept VISA, MasterCard, and American Express

Order by Mail
- Send the full price of your order (MN residents add 7% sales tax)
  in U.S. funds, plus postage & handling to:

  Llewellyn Worldwide
  P.O. Box 64383, Dept. 1-56718-446-4
  St. Paul, MN 55164–0383, U.S.A.

Postage & Handling
- Standard (U.S., Mexico, & Canada)

If your order is:
  $20.00 or under, add $5.00
  $20.01–$100.00, add $6.00
  Over $100, shipping is free

(Continental U.S. orders ship UPS. AK, HI, PR, & P.O. Boxes ship USPS 1st class.
Mex. & Can. ship PMB.)

- Second Day Air (Continental U.S. only): $10.00 for one book + $1.00
  per each additional book
- Express (AK, HI, & PR only) [Not available for P.O. Box delivery. For
  street address delivery only.]: $15.00 for one book + $1.00 per each
  additional book
- International Surface Mail: Add $1.00 per item
- International Airmail: Books—Add the retail price of each item;
  Non-book items—Add $5.00 per item

Please allow 4–6 weeks for delivery on all orders. Postage and handling rates subject to change.

Discounts
We offer a 20% discount to group leaders or agents. You must
order a minimum of 5 copies of the same book to get our special
quantity price.

Free Catalog
Get a free copy of our color catalog, New Worlds of Mind and
Spirit. Subscribe for just $10.00 in the United States and
Canada ($30.00 overseas, airmail). Many bookstores carry
New Worlds—ask for it!

Visit our website at www.llewellyn.com for more information.

Bud, Blossom, & Leaf

The Magical Herb Gardener's Handbook

Dorothy Morrison

Here, in one single volume, is everything you need to know about herbs, both the mundane and the magical. Do you want to know how to tend them with hydroponic magic? Use them to clean your home? Or brew them into fine wines fit for the gods? This book not only answers these questions, but takes you on a magical journey down the garden path. Explore theme gardens and shapes to find the one that fits your magical purpose. Learn how to appease the home spirits so your garden will prosper and thrive. Travel outdoors and discover how to balance your garden into its magical best. Then step into the kitchen and whip up soothing ointments, beauty treatments, culinary delights, pest control solutions, and housecleaning supplies.

Packed with 125 spells, invocations, rituals, and recipes, Bud, Blossom & Leaf *guides you on the path to becoming a magical herb gardener:*

- Learn how to predict the weather and choose the best time frames for the gardening process
- Explore magical garden themes, garden shapes, and planting ideas
- Plant and grow a magical herb garden indoors or out
- Try out recipes for culinary, cosmetic, and first aid uses

1-56718-443-X, 192 pp., 7½ x 9⅛, illus.   **$14.95**

To order, call 1-800-THE MOON

Prices subject to change without notice

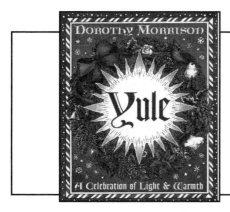

Yule
A Celebration of Light & Warmth

Dorothy Morrison

The "holidays": some call them Christmas or Hanukkah, others know them as Los Posadas or Ta Dhiu. Still others celebrate Winter Solstice or Yule. They are a time for reflection, resolution, and renewal. Whatever our beliefs, the holidays provide us with rituals to celebrate the balance of light and dark, and for welcoming the healing powers of warmth back into our world.

Jam packed with more than sixty spells, invocations, and rituals, *Yule* guides you through the magic of the season. Traveling its realm will bring back the joy you felt as a child—the spirit of warmth and good will that lit the long winter nights. Discover the origin of the eight tiny reindeer, brew up some Yuletide coffee, and learn ways to create your own holiday traditions and crafts based on celebrations from a variety of countries and beliefs.

1-56718-496-0, 216 pp., 7½ x 9⅛, 56 illus. $17.95

To order, call 1-800-THE MOON
Prices subject to change without notice

Everyday Magic
Spells & Rituals for Modern Living

Dorothy Morrison

Are you tired of looking for ritual solutions for today's problems: computer viruses, traffic that drives you crazy, and stress that makes you forget your own name? Does the quest for obscure spell ingredients leave you exhausted and empty-handed?

Now there's a better way to incorporate magic into your life *without* adding more stress to it. *Everyday Magic* updates the ancient arts to fit today's lifestyle. It promotes the use of modern convenience items as viable magical tools, and it incorporates the use of easy-to-find spell ingredients—most of which are already in your kitchen cabinet. It discusses the items and forces that boost magical work, as well as a multitude of time-saving tips and a large assortment of recipes for creating your own oils, incenses, potions, and powders. More than 300 spells and rituals cover the everyday concerns of the modern practitioner.

- Set your spell into motion and speed up the results with "magical boosters"
- Magnify your focused intent and energy flow with herbs, flowers, trees, and stones
- Learn how to perform ancient arts with modern tools: your coffee maker, blender, and crock pot
- Make your own magical powders, sachets, bath salts, potpourris, incenses, and oils
- Discover the secret to success in magical workings
- Practice spells for more than 300 purposes

1-56718-469-3, 304 pp., 5³⁄₁₆ x 8 $9.95

To order, call 1-800-THE MOON

Prices subject to change without notice

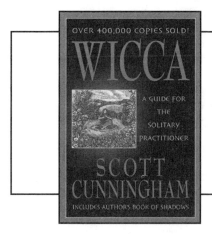

Wicca
A Guide for the Solitary Practitioner
Scott Cunningham

Wicca is a book of life, and how to live magically, spiritually, and wholly attuned with Nature. It is a book of sense and common sense, not only about Magick, but about religion and one of the most critical issues of today: how to achieve the much needed and wholesome relationship with our Earth. Cunningham presents Wicca as it is today: a gentle, Earth-oriented religion dedicated to the Goddess and God. This book fulfills a need for a practical guide to solitary Wicca—a need which no previous book has fulfilled.

Here is a positive, practical introduction to the religion of Wicca, designed so that any interested person can learn to practice the religion alone, anywhere in the world. It presents Wicca honestly and clearly, without the pseudo-history that permeates other books. It shows that Wicca is a vital, satisfying part of twentieth- century life.

This book presents the theory and practice of Wicca from an individual's perspective. The section on the Standing Stones Book of Shadows contains solitary rituals for the Esbats and Sabbats. This book, based on the author's nearly two decades of Wiccan practice, presents an eclectic picture of various aspects of this religion. Exercises designed to develop magical proficiency, a self-dedication ritual, herb, crystal and rune magic, as well as recipes for Sabbat feasts, are included in this excellent book.

0-87542-118-0, 240 pp., 6 x 9, illus. $9.95

To order, call 1-800-THE MOON
Prices subject to change without notice

Buckland's Complete Book of Witchcraft

Raymond Buckland

Here is the most complete resource to the study and practice of modern, nondenominational Wicca. This is a lavishly illustrated, self-study course for the solitary or group. Included are rituals; exercises for developing psychic talents; information on all major "sects" of the Craft; sections on tools, beliefs, dreams, meditations, divination, herbal lore, healing, ritual clothing; and much, much more. This book unites theory and practice into a comprehensive course designed to help you develop into a practicing Witch, one of the "Wise Ones." It is written by Ray Buckland, a very famous and respected authority on Witchcraft who first came public with the Old Religion in the United States. Large format with workbook-type exercises, profusely illustrated and full of music and chants. Takes you from A to Z in the study of Witchcraft.

Never before has so much information on the Craft of the Wise been collected in one place. Traditionally, there are three degrees of advancement in most Wiccan traditions. When you have completed studying this book, you will be the equivalent of a Third-Degree Witch. Even those who have practiced Wicca for years find useful information in this book, and many covens are using this for their textbook. If you want to become a Witch, or if you merely want to find out what Witchcraft is really about, you will find no better book than this.

0-87542-050-8, 272 pp., 8½ x 11, illus.   **$16.95**

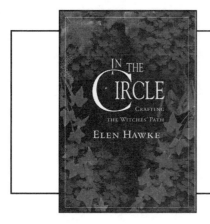

In the Circle
Crafting the Witches' Path

Elen Hawke

Are you new to witchcraft, or are you looking for fresh ideas to enliven your practice? Whatever your age or level of experience, this book is for you. Take a step-by-step journey through the Moon's phases, the eight seasonal festivals, an understanding of Goddess and God, building a shrine, collecting or making magical tools, performing ritual, exploring sacred sites, and many other aspects of modern witchcraft.

Containing nearly thirty beautiful illustrations, *In The Circle* combines Elen Hawke's personal accounts of sabbats and moon rites with a clear, common-sense approach that makes witchcraft accessible to anyone. Whether you want to practice alone, with a partner, or in a group, In the Circle will be a wise guide, providing answers that are inspirational and empowering. Each section takes you deeper into your inner core, the place where you can connect to the spirit of Nature and to your innate knowledge.

For advanced students, this book will rekindle your interest in and love for the Craft, reminding you of why you began practicing witchcraft in the first place.

- Learn how to apply the practical tools of the Craft to shape a way of working that is both rewarding and sacred
- Discover how another witch experiences ritual and the wheel of the year
- Get thoughtful answers to almost every beginning-level question you might have

1-56718-444-8, 192 pp., 6 x 9, 27 illus. $12.95

To order, call 1-800-THE MOON
Prices subject to change without notice